Conference on Empirical Methods in Natural Language Processing (EMNLP 2024)

Tutorial Abstracts

Miami, Florida, USA
12-16 November 2024

ISBN: 979-8-3313-0840-7

Printed from e-media with permission by:

Curran Associates, Inc.
57 Morehouse Lane
Red Hook, NY 12571

Some format issues inherent in the e-media version may also appear in this print version.

Printed with permission by Curran Associates, Inc. (2025)

For permission requests, please contact the Association for Computational Linguistics at the address below.

Association for Computational Linguistics
209 N. Eighth Street
Stroudsburg, Pennsylvania 18360

Phone: 1-570-476-8006
Fax: 1-570-476-0860

acl@aclweb.org

Additional copies of this publication are available from:

Curran Associates, Inc.
57 Morehouse Lane
Red Hook, NY 12571 USA
Phone: 845-758-0400
Fax: 845-758-2633
Email: curran@proceedings.com
Web: www.proceedings.com

EMNLP 2024

The 2024 Conference on Empirical Methods in Natural Language Processing

Tutorial Abstracts

November 12–16, 2024

Order copies of this and other ACL proceedings from:

Association for Computational Linguistics (ACL)
317 Sidney Baker St. S
Suite 400 - 134
Kerrville, TX 78028
USA
Tel: +1-855-225-1962
acl@aclweb.org

Introduction

Welcome to the Tutorial Session of EMNLP 2024!

As the field of NLP continues to evolve, this year's tutorials at EMNLP 2024 will give the audience comprehensive introductions of six exciting topics by experts in these areas: natural language explanations, offensive speech, human-centered evaluation, AI for science, agents, and enhancing capabilities of LLMs.

As in recent years, the process of calling for, submitting, reviewing, and selecting tutorials was a collaborative effort across ACL, EACL, NAACL, and EMNLP. Each tutorial proposal was meticulously reviewed by a panel of three reviewers, who assessed them based on criteria such as clarity, preparedness, novelty, timeliness, instructors' experience, potential audience, open access to teaching materials, and diversity (including multilingualism, gender, age, and geolocation). A total of six tutorials covering the aforementioned topics were selected for EMNLP.

We would like to thank the tutorial authors for their contributions, the tutorial chairs across conferences for this coordinated effort, as well as the EMNLP conference organizers, especially the general chair Thamar Solorio.

EMNLP 2024 Tutorial Co-chairs
Junyi Jessy Li
Fei Liu

Organizing Committee

General Chair

Thamar Solorio, Mohamed bin Zayed University of Artificial Intelligence and University of Houston

Program Chairs

Yaser Al-Onaizan, Saudi Data and AI Authority, National Center for AI

Mohit Bansal, University of North Carolina at Chapel Hill

Yun-Nung (Vivian) Chen, National Taiwan University

Tutorial Chairs

Jessy Li, The University of Texas at Austin

Fei Liu, Emory University

Table of Contents

Program

Friday, November 15

09:00–12:30 *Enhancing LLM Capabilities Beyond Scaling Up*
Wenpeng Yin, Muhao Chen, Rui Zhang, Ben Zhou, Fei Wang and Dan Roth

09:00–12:30 *Countering Hateful and Offensive Speech Online - Open Challenges*
Leon Derczynski, Marco Guerini, Debora Nozza, Flor Miriam Plaza-del-Arco, Jeffrey Sorensen and Marcos Zampieri

14:00–17:30 *Language Agents: Foundations, Prospects, and Risks*
Yu Su, Diyi Yang, Shunyu Yao and Tao Yu

14:00–17:30 *Introductory Tutorial: Reasoning with Natural Language Explanations*
Marco Valentino and André Freitas

Saturday, November 16

09:00–12:30 *AI for Science in the Era of Large Language Models*
Zhenyu Bi, Minghao Xu, Jian Tang and Xuan Wang

14:00–17:30 *Human-Centered Evaluation of Language Technologies*
Su Lin Blodgett, Jackie Chi Kit Cheung, Vera Liao and Ziang Xiao

Enhancing LLM Capabilities Beyond Scaling Up

Wenpeng Yin[†], **Muhao Chen**[♠‡], **Rui Zhang**[†], **Ben Zhou**[⋆], **Fei Wang**[‡], **Dan Roth**[◇♯]
[†]Penn State; [♠]UC Davis; [⋆]ASU; [‡]USC; [◇]Oracle; [♯]UPenn
{wenpeng,rmz5227}@psu.edu; muhchen@ucdavis.edu
benzhou@asu.edu; fwang598@usc.edu; danroth@seas.upenn.edu

Abstract

General-purpose large language models (LLMs) are progressively expanding both in scale and access to unpublic training data. This has led to notable progress in a variety of AI problems. Nevertheless, two questions exist: i) Is scaling up the sole avenue of extending the capabilities of LLMs? ii) Instead of developing general-purpose LLMs, how to endow LLMs with specific knowledge? This tutorial targets researchers and practitioners who are interested in capability extension of LLMs that go beyond scaling up. To this end, we will discuss several lines of research that follow that direction, including: (i) optimizing input prompts to fully exploit LLM potential, (ii) enabling LLMs to self-improve responses through various feedback signals, (iii) updating or editing the internal knowledge of LLMs when necessary, (iv) leveraging incidental structural supervision from target tasks, and (v) defending against potential attacks and threats from malicious users. At last, we will conclude the tutorial by outlining directions for further investigation.[1]

1 Introduction

The advancement of AI can be broadly attributed to two technical trajectories: one involving general-purpose models, and the other centering around task-specific models. In the earlier phases of deep learning and even before its inception, the focal point of research predominantly revolved around the integration of domain-specific and task-specific expertise into model architectures. Nonetheless, the landscape underwent a transformation with the advent of pretrained large language models (LLMs), e.g., BERT (Devlin et al., 2019) and GPT series (OpenAI, 2022, 2023). Recent years have witnessed substantial achievements of those general-purpose models in a variety of AI problems. However, the advancements facilitated by LLMs are primarily rooted in larger scales of model parameters and confidential training data. These factors make LLMs increasingly costly, uninterpretable, unreproducible, uncontrollable, and unmanageable for most users.

Consequently, while acknowledging the substantial benefits offered by LLMs, it becomes crucial to address several pertinent inquiries. Firstly, *does the path to enhancing LLMs' capabilities solely involve scaling up?* The resource-intensive nature of training large-scale LLMs prompts the exploration of potential bottlenecks and the feasibility of further expansion. Secondly, *despite LLMs' versatility, challenges persist in their application to specific disciplines, tasks, and even users*. Thus, strategies to augment LLMs' capabilities for these distinctive challenges warrant consideration.

This tutorial delves into some research lines that extend the capabilities of LLMs beyond mere scale amplification. Specifically, it presents a comprehensive analysis of this objective, identifying challenges across five key dimensions: *optimizing LLM inputs*, *enhancing LLM responses*, *updating LLMs' internal knowledge*, *maximizing supervision from the target task*, and *improving LLM trustworthiness*. In line with these dimensions, the tutorial will address recent advancements in: (i) prompt optimization (§2.2), (ii) LLM self-improvement and inter-LLM collaboration (§2.3), (iii) adapting pre-existing knowledge to integrate new, potentially conflicting information (§2.4), (iv) aligning LLM performance with the constraints and structures of target problems (§2.5), and (v) defending against adversarial threats and malicious attacks (§2.6).

We believe it is necessary to present a timely tutorial to comprehensively summarize the new frontiers in LLM capability extension research and point out the emerging challenges that deserve further investigation. Participants will learn about

[1]Materials available at www.wenpengyin.org/publications/beyond-llm-scaling-emnlp24

Proceedings of the 2024 Conference on Empirical Methods in Natural Language Processing: Tutorial Abstracts, pages 1–10
November 12–16, 2024.

recent trends, emerging challenges, and representative tools in this topic, and how related technologies benefit end-user NLP applications.

2 Outline of Tutorial Content

This **half-day** tutorial presents a systematic overview of recent advancements in extending LLMs' capabilities without scaling up. The detailed contents are outlined below.

2.1 Background and Motivation

We will begin motivating this topic with a selection of real-world applications and emerging challenges of general-purpose LLMs.

2.2 Prompt Optimization for LLMs

Large Language Models (LLMs) have shown remarkable performance across a wide range of tasks. However, they are known to be sensitive to prompt variations, where even slight changes in input can cause substantial differences in output quality (Lu et al., 2021). As a result, effective prompt design has become essential for maximizing LLM performance. Despite this, finding the optimal prompts still often involves manual trial and error, which demands considerable human effort and can yield suboptimal results (Wei et al., 2022; Kojima et al., 2022). In this section, we will introduce several emerging techniques of prompt optimization for LLMs, which aim to systematically search for prompts that improve target task performance. We organize our discussion into several categories including search-based prompt optimization (Prasad et al., 2022; Guo et al., 2023; Schnabel and Neville, 2024), text gradient–based prompt optimization (Pryzant et al., 2023; Ye et al., 2023; Yuksekgonul et al., 2024), and gradient-based prompt optimization (Wen et al., 2024). We will conclude this section by presenting several promising future directions such as prompt optimization for multiagent LLMs, optimization for long and complex prompts, prompt optimization by retrieving and augmenting domain knowledge, human-in-the-loop interactive prompt optimization, and theoretical analysis of prompt optimization.

2.3 LLM Self-improvement & LLM-LLM Collaboration

In this subsection, we provide a detailed discussion on how LLMs can harness their own capabilities for self-improvement or collaborate with peer LLMs to address more complex problems.

The concept of LLM self-improvement has garnered increasing attention in recent literature (Kamoi et al., 2024; Pan et al., 2023b). On one hand, a growing body of work has demonstrated the potential of self-improvement strategies (Kumar et al., 2024; Kim et al., 2023; Huang et al., 2023b; Patel et al., 2024; Jiang et al., 2024a), including techniques like self-feedback (Madaan et al., 2023) and self-discriminative abilities (Ahn et al., 2024). On the other hand, some studies have questioned the effectiveness of these self-improvement mechanisms (Stechly et al., 2023; Huang et al., 2024; Jiang et al., 2024b; Valmeekam et al., 2023).

In addition to exploring the limits of individual LLM capabilities, we also examine recent advancements in combining multiple LLMs. These include: i) LLM-LLM collaboration, such as detecting factual errors through cross-examination (Cohen et al., 2023), multi-agent cooperation (Du et al., 2024; Talebirad and Nadiri, 2023), and LLM control of other AI agents (Shen et al., 2023); ii) LLM-LLM merging, which aims to produce a new, singular "super" LLM (Tam et al., 2024; Tam et al.; Liu et al., 2024a; Goddard et al., 2024; Perin et al., 2024).

2.4 Knowledge Update of LLMs

LLMs encapsulate vast world knowledge acquired during pre-training, yet the ever-evolving nature of information often results in *outdated or biased knowledge*, potentially leading to the dissemination of misinformation. In this section, we first examine the issues caused by unreliable knowledge, such as hallucinations (Xu et al., 2024c; Longpre et al., 2021; Li et al., 2023a; Wang et al., 2023c). Next, we explore approaches to remedy knowledge gaps in LLMs' internal knowledge by integrating external information in a training-free manner. We begin by enforcing LLMs' reliance on external context when the external knowledge is verified as reliable (Wang et al., 2023a; Zhou et al., 2023). We then address more general and realistic scenarios where both internal and external knowledge may be noisy, discussing effective strategies for combining these sources (Zhang et al.; Zhao et al., 2024). Finally, we introduce techniques for knowledge editing in LLMs with lightweight tuning (Lin et al., 2024; Wang et al., 2024c; Huang et al., 2023a).

2.5 Aligning with Structures of Target Problems

Aligning models with pre-defined structures is an efficient method of improving model performances without scaling up. During this process, models adapt to structures that are beneficial to solving target problems and produce outputs that are more consistent with expectations. We discuss three types of such structures in this section. The first type uses symbolic constraints as structures, which include human-written constraints (Wang et al., 2024b), mathematical constraints (Feng et al., 2024), and compiler constraints (Chen et al., 2023; Zhu et al., 2024). The second type finds structures from decomposing the target problem (Sun et al., 2023; Chen et al., 2024b; Zhou et al., 2024b; Wu and Xie, 2024). The last type of structures are procedural structures that come from cognitive or problem-solving processes, such as DSP (Khattab et al., 2022), ReAct (Yao et al., 2022), and RAP (Hao et al., 2023). These procedural structures can also be combined with symbolic constraints (Pan et al., 2023a), task decompositions (Hu et al., 2023; LYU et al., 2023), or both (Zhou et al., 2024a).

2.6 Safety Enhancement for LLMs

Despite the desire to align LLM responses with users' preferences, malicious data may exist in the training corpora, task instructions, and human feedback. These data are likely to cause threats to LLMs before they are deployed as services (Wan et al., 2023; Xu et al., 2024a; Greshake et al., 2023). Due to the limited accessibility of model components in these services, mitigating such threats needs to be addressed through inference-time defense rather than training-time safety enhancement (Wang et al., 2024a). In this part of the tutorial, we will first introduce **inference-time threats** to LLMs through prompt injection, malicious task instructions, jailbreaking attacks, adversarial demonstrations, and training-free backdoor attacks (Liu et al., 2023b; Xu et al., 2024a; Li et al., 2023b; Wang et al., 2023b; Huang et al., 2023c; Greshake et al., 2023; Xu et al., 2024b). We will then provide insights on mitigating some of those threats based on **defense techniques** including prompt robustness estimation, demonstration-based defense and ensemble debiasing (Liu et al., 2023a, 2024b; Graf et al., 2024; Wu et al., 2023), defensive demonstrations (Mo et al., 2023), or detection techniques where defenders can detect and eliminate poisoned data given the compromised model (Kurita et al., 2020; Chen and Dai, 2021; Qi et al., 2021; Li et al., 2021, 2023c). While many issues with inference-time threats remain unaddressed (Chen et al., 2024a). We will also provide a discussion about how the community should develop to combat those issues.

2.7 Future Research Directions

Enhancing general-purpose large language models (LLMs) with specialized capabilities tailored to specific datasets, problems, and user requirements is essential for their effective deployment in real-world applications. We conclude this tutorial by discussing several ongoing challenges and promising avenues for future research, including: (i) adapting LLMs to different scientific disciplines to model complex processes (Jadhav et al., 2024; Thirunavukarasu et al., 2023), (ii) employing Mixture of Experts architectures (Sukhbaatar et al., 2024; Xue et al., 2024), (iii) exploring novel approaches for constructing foundational models that transcend Transformer-based generative AI, such as Liquid Foundation Models [2], and (iv) advancing autonomous systems for goal planning, action execution, and self-evolution through continuous learning (Crowder et al., 2020).

3 Specification of the Tutorial

The proposed tutorial is considered a **cutting-edge** tutorial that introduces new frontiers in LLM capability extension beyond scaling up its size and data. The presented topic has not been covered by any *CL tutorials in the past 4 years.

Audience and Prerequisites Based on the level of interest in this topic, we expect around 250 participants. While no specific background knowledge is assumed of the audience, it would be best for the attendees to know about basic deep learning technologies, pre-trained language models (e.g. encoder-based LLMs and decoder-based LLMs). A reading list that could help provide background knowledge to the audience before attending this tutorial is given in Appx. §A.2.

Breadth We estimate that at least 60% of the work covered in this tutorial is from researchers other than the instructors of the tutorial.

Diversity Considerations This tutorial will explore cutting-edge research on updating and adapting LLMs with new knowledge, user preferences, constraints, defense techniques, task capabilities,

[2] `https://www.liquid.ai/liquid-foundation-models`

and external tools/models. The team includes a senior Ph.D. student and several assistant and distinguished professors, and will promote the tutorial on social media to broaden audience participation.

4 Tutorial Instructors

The following are biographies of the speakers. Past tutorials given by us are listed in Appx. §A.1.

Wenpeng Yin is an Assistant Professor in the Department of Computer Science and Engineering at Penn State University. Prior to joining Penn State, he was a tenure-track faculty member at Temple University (1/2022-12/2022), Senior Research Scientist at Salesforce Research (8/2019-12/2021), a postdoctoral researcher at UPenn (10/2017-7/2019), and got his Ph.D. degree from the Ludwig Maximilian University of Munich, Germany, in 2017. Dr. Yin's research focuses on natural language processing with three sub-areas: (i) NLP/LLM for scientific research, (ii) human-centered AI, and (iii) multimodal learning. Additional information is available at `www.wenpengyin.org`.

Muhao Chen is an assistant professor in the Department of Computer Science at UC Davis, where he directs the Language Understanding and Knowledge Acquisition (LUKA) Group. His research focuses on data-driven machine learning approaches for natural language understanding and knowledge acquisition. His work has been recognized with an NSF CRII Award, two Amazon Research Awards, a Cisco Faculty Research Award, an EMNLP Outstanding Paper Award, and an ACM SIGBio Best Student Paper Award. Muhao obtained his PhD degree from UCLA Department of Computer Science in 2019, was a postdoctoral researcher at UPenn, and worked as as Assistant Research Professor of Computer Science at USC prior to joining UC Davis. Additional information is available at `http://luka-group.github.io`.

Rui Zhang is an Assistant Professor in the Computer Science and Engineering Department of Penn State University and a co-director of the PSU NLP Lab. His overarching research goal is to build natural language interfaces for efficient information access and knowledge sharing including summarization for unstructured documents, question answering for semi-structured web tables and pages, and semantic parsing for structured knowledge. He has led a tutorial on contrastive data and learning for natural language processing at NAACL 2022. He is the co-organizer of several workshops including SUKI at NAACL 2022, MIA at NAACL 2022, and IntEx-SemPar at EMNLP 2020. Additional information is available at `https://ryanzhumich.github.io/`.

Ben Zhou is an Assistant Professor in the School of Computing and Augmented Intelligence at Arizona State University. Ben's research uses data and symbolic cognitive processes to improve model reasoning, controllability, and trustworthiness from learning/inference schemes and architectural perspectives. He has more than 10 recent papers on related topics. Ben obtained his Ph.D. degree from the University of Pennsylvania. He is a recipient of the ENIAC fellowship from the University of Pennsylvania and a finalist for the CRA Outstanding Undergraduate Researcher Award. Additional information is available at `http://xuanyu.me/`.

Fei Wang is a Ph.D. student in the Department of Computer Science at University of Southern California. His research interests lie in natural language processing and machine learning. His recent work focuses on enhancing the trustworthiness of LLMs with dynamic knowledge integration and robust alignment. Fei is a recipient of an Amazon ML Fellowship and an Annenberg Fellowship. Additional information is available at `https://feiwang96.github.io/`.

Dan Roth is the Eduardo D. Glandt Distinguished Professor at the Department of Computer and Information Science, UPenn, the Chief AI Scientist at Oracle, and a Fellow of the AAAS, ACM, AAAI, and ACL. In 2017, Roth was awarded the John McCarthy Award, the highest award the AI community gives to mid-career AI researchers. Roth was recognized "for major conceptual and theoretical advances in the modeling of natural language understanding, machine learning, and reasoning." Roth has published broadly in machine learning, NLP, KRR, and learning theory, and has given keynote talks and tutorials in all ACL and AAAI major conferences. Roth was the Editor-in-Chief of JAIR until 2017, and was the program chair of AAAI'11, ACL'03 and CoNLL'02; he serves regularly as an area chair and senior program committee member in the major conferences in his research areas. Additional information is available at `www.cis.upenn.edu/~danroth`.

Ethical Considerations

We do not anticipate any ethical issues particularly to the topics of the tutorial. Nevertheless, some work presented in this tutorial extensively uses large-scale pretrained models with self-attention, which may lead to substantial financial and environmental costs.

Acknowledgment

Muhao Chen was supported by the DARPA FoundSci Grant HR00112490370, the NSF of the United States Grant ITE 2333736 and an Amazon Research Award. Fei Wang was supported by the Amazon ML Fellowship.

References

Jihyun Janice Ahn, Ryo Kamoi, Lu Cheng, Rui Zhang, and Wenpeng Yin. 2024. Direct-inverse prompting: Analyzing llms' discriminative capacity in self-improving generation. *CoRR*, abs/2407.11017.

Chuanshuai Chen and Jiazhu Dai. 2021. Mitigating backdoor attacks in LSTM-based text classification systems by backdoor keyword identification. *Neurocomputing*, 452:253–262.

Muhao Chen, Chaowei Xiao, Huan Sun, Lei Li, Leon Derczynski, Anima Anandkumar, and Fei Wang. 2024a. Combating security and privacy issues in the era of large language models. In *Proceedings of the 2024 Conference of the North American Chapter of the Association for Computational Linguistics: Human Language Technologies (Volume 5: Tutorial Abstracts)*, pages 8–18, Mexico City, Mexico. Association for Computational Linguistics.

Sihao Chen, Hongming Zhang, Tong Chen, Ben Zhou, Wenhao Yu, Dian Yu, Baolin Peng, Hongwei Wang, Dan Roth, and Dong Yu. 2024b. Sub-sentence encoder: Contrastive learning of propositional semantic representations. In *Proceedings of the 2024 Conference of the North American Chapter of the Association for Computational Linguistics: Human Language Technologies (Volume 1: Long Papers)*, pages 1596–1609.

Xinyun Chen, Maxwell Lin, Nathanael Schärli, and Denny Zhou. 2023. Teaching large language models to self-debug. *ArXiv*, abs/2304.05128.

Roi Cohen, May Hamri, Mor Geva, and Amir Globerson. 2023. LM vs LM: detecting factual errors via cross examination. In *Proceedings of the 2023 Conference on Empirical Methods in Natural Language Processing, EMNLP 2023, Singapore, December 6-10, 2023*, pages 12621–12640. Association for Computational Linguistics.

James A Crowder, John Carbone, Shelli Friess, James A Crowder, John Carbone, and Shelli Friess. 2020. Artificial creativity and self-evolution: Abductive reasoning in artificial life forms. *Artificial Psychology: Psychological Modeling and Testing of AI Systems*, pages 65–74.

Jacob Devlin, Ming-Wei Chang, Kenton Lee, and Kristina Toutanova. 2019. BERT: pre-training of deep bidirectional transformers for language understanding. In *Proceedings of NAACL-HLT*, pages 4171–4186. Association for Computational Linguistics.

Yilun Du, Shuang Li, Antonio Torralba, Joshua B. Tenenbaum, and Igor Mordatch. 2024. Improving factuality and reasoning in language models through multiagent debate. In *Forty-first International Conference on Machine Learning, ICML 2024, Vienna, Austria, July 21-27, 2024*. OpenReview.net.

Yu Feng, Ben Zhou, Weidong Lin, and Dan Roth. 2024. Bird: A trustworthy bayesian inference framework for large language models. *arXiv preprint arXiv:2404.12494*.

Charles Goddard, Shamane Siriwardhana, Malikeh Ehghaghi, Luke Meyers, Vlad Karpukhin, Brian Benedict, Mark McQuade, and Jacob Solawetz. 2024. Arcee's mergekit: A toolkit for merging large language models. *CoRR*, abs/2403.13257.

Victoria Graf, Qin Liu, and Muhao Chen. 2024. Two heads are better than one: Nested poe for robust defense against multi-backdoors. In *NAACL*.

Kai Greshake, Sahar Abdelnabi, Shailesh Mishra, Christoph Endres, Thorsten Holz, and Mario Fritz. 2023. More than you've asked for: A comprehensive analysis of novel prompt injection threats to application-integrated large language models. *arXiv preprint arXiv:2302.12173*.

Qingyan Guo, Rui Wang, Junliang Guo, Bei Li, Kaitao Song, Xu Tan, Guoqing Liu, Jiang Bian, and Yujiu Yang. 2023. Connecting large language models with evolutionary algorithms yields powerful prompt optimizers. *arXiv preprint arXiv:2309.08532*.

Shibo Hao, Yi Gu, Haodi Ma, Joshua Hong, Zhen Wang, Daisy Wang, and Zhiting Hu. 2023. Reasoning with language model is planning with world model. In *Proceedings of the 2023 Conference on Empirical Methods in Natural Language Processing*, pages 8154–8173.

Y. Hu, Haotong Yang, Zhouchen Lin, and Muhan Zhang. 2023. Code prompting: a neural symbolic method for complex reasoning in large language models. *ArXiv*, abs/2305.18507.

James Y. Huang, Wenxuan Zhou, Fei Wang, Fred Morstatter, Sheng Zhang, Hoifung Poon, and Muhao Chen. 2023a. Offset unlearning for large language models. *arXiv preprint arXiv:2311.09763*.

Jiaxin Huang, Shixiang Gu, Le Hou, Yuexin Wu, Xuezhi Wang, Hongkun Yu, and Jiawei Han. 2023b. Large language models can self-improve. In *Proceedings of the 2023 Conference on Empirical Methods in Natural Language Processing, EMNLP 2023, Singapore, December 6-10, 2023*, pages 1051–1068. Association for Computational Linguistics.

Jie Huang, Xinyun Chen, Swaroop Mishra, Huaixiu Steven Zheng, Adams Wei Yu, Xinying Song, and Denny Zhou. 2024. Large language models cannot self-correct reasoning yet. In *The Twelfth International Conference on Learning Representations, ICLR 2024, Vienna, Austria, May 7-11, 2024*. OpenReview.net.

Yujin Huang, Terry Yue Zhuo, Qiongkai Xu, Han Hu, Xingliang Yuan, and Chunyang Chen. 2023c. Training-free lexical backdoor attacks on language models. In *Proceedings of the ACM Web Conference 2023*, pages 2198–2208.

Yayati Jadhav, Peter Pak, and Amir Barati Farimani. 2024. Llm-3d print: Large language models to monitor and control 3d printing. *arXiv preprint arXiv:2408.14307*.

Chunyang Jiang, Chi-Min Chan, Wei Xue, Qifeng Liu, and Yike Guo. 2024a. Importance weighting can help large language models self-improve. *CoRR*, abs/2408.09849.

Dongwei Jiang, Jingyu Zhang, Orion Weller, Nathaniel Weir, Benjamin Van Durme, and Daniel Khashabi. 2024b. Self-[in]correct: Llms struggle with discriminating self-generated responses.

Ryo Kamoi, Yusen Zhang, Nan Zhang, Jiawei Han, and Rui Zhang. 2024. When can llms actually correct their own mistakes? A critical survey of self-correction of llms. *Transactions of the Association for Computational Linguistics*, abs/2406.01297.

O. Khattab, Keshav Santhanam, Xiang Lisa Li, David Leo Wright Hall, Percy Liang, Christopher Potts, and Matei A. Zaharia. 2022. Demonstrate-search-predict: Composing retrieval and language models for knowledge-intensive nlp. *ArXiv*, abs/2212.14024.

Taehyeon Kim, Joonkee Kim, Gihun Lee, and Se-Young Yun. 2023. Distort, distract, decode: Instruction-tuned model can refine its response from noisy instructions. *CoRR*, abs/2311.00233.

Takeshi Kojima, Shixiang Shane Gu, Machel Reid, Yutaka Matsuo, and Yusuke Iwasawa. 2022. Large language models are zero-shot reasoners. *Advances in neural information processing systems*, 35:22199–22213.

Aviral Kumar, Vincent Zhuang, Rishabh Agarwal, Yi Su, John D Co-Reyes, Avi Singh, Kate Baumli, Shariq Iqbal, Colton Bishop, Rebecca Roelofs, et al. 2024. Training language models to self-correct via reinforcement learning. *arXiv preprint arXiv:2409.12917*.

Keita Kurita, Paul Michel, and Graham Neubig. 2020. Weight poisoning attacks on pretrained models. In *Proceedings of the 58th Annual Meeting of the Association for Computational Linguistics*, pages 2793–2806, Online. Association for Computational Linguistics.

Bangzheng Li, Ben Zhou, Fei Wang, Xingyu Fu, Dan Roth, and Muhao Chen. 2023a. Deceiving semantic shortcuts on reasoning chains: How far can models go without hallucination? In *Proceedings of NAACL 2023*.

Haoran Li, Dadi Guo, Wei Fan, Mingshi Xu, and Yangqiu Song. 2023b. Multi-step jailbreaking privacy attacks on chatgpt. *arXiv preprint arXiv:2304.05197*.

Jiazhao Li, Zhuofeng Wu, Wei Ping, Chaowei Xiao, and VG Vydiswaran. 2023c. Defending against insertion-based textual backdoor attacks via attribution. *arXiv preprint arXiv:2305.02394*.

Zichao Li, Dheeraj Mekala, Chengyu Dong, and Jingbo Shang. 2021. BFClass: A backdoor-free text classification framework. In *Findings of the Association for Computational Linguistics: EMNLP 2021*, pages 444–453, Punta Cana, Dominican Republic. Association for Computational Linguistics.

Zihao Lin, Mohammad Beigi, Hongxuan Li, Yufan Zhou, Yuxiang Zhang, Qifan Wang, Wenpeng Yin, and Lifu Huang. 2024. Navigating the dual facets: A comprehensive evaluation of sequential memory editing in large language models. In *Proceedings of the 62nd Annual Meeting of the Association for Computational Linguistics (Volume 1: Long Papers)*, pages 13755–13772, Bangkok, Thailand. Association for Computational Linguistics.

Deyuan Liu, Zecheng Wang, Bingning Wang, Weipeng Chen, Chunshan Li, Zhiying Tu, Dianhui Chu, Bo Li, and Dianbo Sui. 2024a. Checkpoint merging via bayesian optimization in LLM pretraining. *CoRR*, abs/2403.19390.

Qin Liu, Fei Wang, Chaowei Xiao, and Muhao Chen. 2024b. From shortcuts to triggers: Backdoor defense with denoised poe. In *NAACL*.

Xiaogeng Liu Liu, Shengshan Hu Hu, Muhao Chen, and Chaowei Xiao. 2023a. Pred: Label-only test-time textual trigger detection. In *EMNLP (in submission)*.

Yi Liu, Gelei Deng, Yuekang Li, Kailong Wang, Tianwei Zhang, Yepang Liu, Haoyu Wang, Yan Zheng, and Yang Liu. 2023b. Prompt injection attack against llm-integrated applications. *arXiv preprint arXiv:2306.05499*.

Shayne Longpre, Kartik Perisetla, Anthony Chen, Nikhil Ramesh, Chris DuBois, and Sameer Singh. 2021. Entity-based knowledge conflicts in question answering. In *Proceedings of the 2021 Conference on Empirical Methods in Natural Language Processing*, pages 7052–7063.

Yao Lu, Max Bartolo, Alastair Moore, Sebastian Riedel, and Pontus Stenetorp. 2021. Fantastically ordered prompts and where to find them: Overcoming few-shot prompt order sensitivity. *arXiv preprint arXiv:2104.08786*.

QING LYU, Shreya Havaldar, Adam Stein, Li Zhang, Delip Rao, Eric Wong, Marianna Apidianaki, and Chris Callison-Burch. 2023. Faithful chain-of-thought reasoning. *ArXiv*, abs/2301.13379.

Aman Madaan, Niket Tandon, Prakhar Gupta, Skyler Hallinan, Luyu Gao, Sarah Wiegreffe, Uri Alon, Nouha Dziri, Shrimai Prabhumoye, Yiming Yang, Shashank Gupta, Bodhisattwa Prasad Majumder, Katherine Hermann, Sean Welleck, Amir Yazdanbakhsh, and Peter Clark. 2023. Self-refine: Iterative refinement with self-feedback. In *Advances in Neural Information Processing Systems 36: Annual Conference on Neural Information Processing Systems 2023, NeurIPS 2023, New Orleans, LA, USA, December 10 - 16, 2023*.

Wenjie Mo, Jiashu Xu, Qin Liu, Jiongxiao Wang, Jun Yan, Chaowei Xiao, and Muhao Chen. 2023. Test-time backdoor mitigation for black-box large language models with defensive demonstrations. *arXiv preprint arXiv:2311.09763*.

OpenAI. 2022. OpenAI: Introducing chatgpt.

OpenAI. 2023. Gpt-4 technical report.

Liangming Pan, Alon Albalak, Xinyi Wang, and William Yang Wang. 2023a. Logic-lm: Empowering large language models with symbolic solvers for faithful logical reasoning. *ArXiv*, abs/2305.12295.

Liangming Pan, Michael Saxon, Wenda Xu, Deepak Nathani, Xinyi Wang, and William Yang Wang. 2023b. Automatically correcting large language models: Surveying the landscape of diverse self-correction strategies. *arXiv preprint arXiv:2308.03188*.

Ajay Patel, Markus Hofmarcher, Claudiu Leoveanu-Condrei, Marius-Constantin Dinu, Chris Callison-Burch, and Sepp Hochreiter. 2024. Large language models can self-improve at web agent tasks. *CoRR*, abs/2405.20309.

Gabriel Perin, Xuxi Chen, Shusen Liu, Bhavya Kailkhura, Zhangyang Wang, and Brian Gallagher. 2024. Rankmean: Module-level importance score for merging fine-tuned LLM models. In *Findings of the Association for Computational Linguistics, ACL 2024, Bangkok, Thailand and virtual meeting, August 11-16, 2024*, pages 1776–1782. Association for Computational Linguistics.

Archiki Prasad, Peter Hase, Xiang Zhou, and Mohit Bansal. 2022. Grips: Gradient-free, edit-based instruction search for prompting large language models. *arXiv preprint arXiv:2203.07281*.

Reid Pryzant, Dan Iter, Jerry Li, Yin Tat Lee, Chenguang Zhu, and Michael Zeng. 2023. Automatic prompt optimization with" gradient descent" and beam search. *arXiv preprint arXiv:2305.03495*.

Fanchao Qi, Yangyi Chen, Mukai Li, Yuan Yao, Zhiyuan Liu, and Maosong Sun. 2021. ONION: A simple and effective defense against textual backdoor attacks. In *Proceedings of the 2021 Conference on Empirical Methods in Natural Language Processing*, pages 9558–9566, Online and Punta Cana, Dominican Republic. Association for Computational Linguistics.

Tobias Schnabel and Jennifer Neville. 2024. Symbolic prompt program search: A structure-aware approach to efficient compile-time prompt optimization.

Yongliang Shen, Kaitao Song, Xu Tan, Dongsheng Li, Weiming Lu, and Yueting Zhuang. 2023. Hugginggpt: Solving AI tasks with chatgpt and its friends in hugging face. In *Advances in Neural Information Processing Systems 36: Annual Conference on Neural Information Processing Systems 2023, NeurIPS 2023, New Orleans, LA, USA, December 10 - 16, 2023*.

Kaya Stechly, Matthew Marquez, and Subbarao Kambhampati. 2023. GPT-4 doesn't know it's wrong: An analysis of iterative prompting for reasoning problems. *CoRR*, abs/2310.12397.

Sainbayar Sukhbaatar, Olga Golovneva, Vasu Sharma, Hu Xu, Xi Victoria Lin, Baptiste Rozière, Jacob Kahn, Daniel Li, Wen-tau Yih, Jason Weston, et al. 2024. Branch-train-mix: Mixing expert llms into a mixture-of-experts llm. *arXiv preprint arXiv:2403.07816*.

Zhiqing Sun, Yikang Shen, Qinhong Zhou, Hongxin Zhang, Zhenfang Chen, David Daniel Cox, Yiming Yang, and Chuang Gan. 2023. Principle-driven self-alignment of language models from scratch with minimal human supervision. In *Thirty-seventh Conference on Neural Information Processing Systems*.

Yashar Talebirad and Amirhossein Nadiri. 2023. Multi-agent collaboration: Harnessing the power of intelligent LLM agents. *CoRR*, abs/2306.03314.

Derek Tam, Mohit Bansal, and Colin Raffel. 2024. Merging by matching models in task parameter subspaces. *Trans. Mach. Learn. Res.*, 2024.

Derek Tam, Margaret Li, Prateek Yadav, Rickard Brüel Gabrielsson, Jiacheng Zhu, Kristjan Greenewald, Mikhail Yurochkin, Mohit Bansal, Colin Raffel, and Leshem Choshen. Llm merging: Building llms efficiently through merging. In *NeurIPS 2024 Competition Track*.

Arun James Thirunavukarasu, Darren Shu Jeng Ting, Kabilan Elangovan, Laura Gutierrez, Ting Fang Tan, and Daniel Shu Wei Ting. 2023. Large language models in medicine. *Nature medicine*, 29(8):1930–1940.

Karthik Valmeekam, Matthew Marquez, and Subbarao Kambhampati. 2023. Can large language models really improve by self-critiquing their own plans? *CoRR*, abs/2310.08118.

Alexander Wan, Eric Wallace, Sheng Shen, and Dan Klein. 2023. Poisoning language models during instruction tuning. *arXiv preprint arXiv:2305.00944*.

Fei Wang, Ninareh Mehrabi, Palash Goyal, Rahul Gupta, Kai-Wei Chang, and Aram Galstyan. 2024a. Data advisor: Dynamic data curation for safety alignment of large language models. In *Proceedings of EMNLP*.

Fei Wang, Wenjie Mo, Yiwei Wang, Wenxuan Zhou, and Muhao Chen. 2023a. A causal view of entity bias in (large) language models. *In submission at EMNLP*.

Fei Wang, Chao Shang, Sarthak Jain, Shuai Wang, Qiang Ning, Bonan Min, Vittorio Castelli, Yassine Benajiba, and Dan Roth. 2024b. From instructions to constraints: Language model alignment with automatic constraint verification. *arXiv preprint arXiv:2403.06326*.

Fei Wang, Wenxuan Zhou, James Y Huang, Nan Xu, Sheng Zhang, Hoifung Poon, and Muhao Chen. 2024c. mdpo: Conditional preference optimization for multimodal large language models.

Jiongxiao Wang, Zichen Liu, Keun Hee Park, Muhao Chen, and Chaowei Xiao. 2023b. Adversarial demonstration attacks on large language models. *arXiv preprint arXiv:2305.14950*.

Yiwei Wang, Bryan Hooi, Fei Wang, Yujun Cai, Yuxuan Liang, Wenxuan Zhou, Jing Tang, Manjuan Duan, and Muhao Chen. 2023c. How fragile is relation extraction under entity replacements? In *Proceedings of the 27th Conference on Computational Natural Language Learning (CoNLL)*, pages 414–423.

Jason Wei, Xuezhi Wang, Dale Schuurmans, Maarten Bosma, Fei Xia, Ed Chi, Quoc V Le, Denny Zhou, et al. 2022. Chain-of-thought prompting elicits reasoning in large language models. *Advances in neural information processing systems*, 35:24824–24837.

Yuxin Wen, Neel Jain, John Kirchenbauer, Micah Goldblum, Jonas Geiping, and Tom Goldstein. 2024. Hard prompts made easy: Gradient-based discrete optimization for prompt tuning and discovery. *Advances in Neural Information Processing Systems*, 36.

Fangzhao Wu, Yueqi Xie, Jingwei Yi, Jiawei Shao, Justin Curl, Lingjuan Lyu, Qifeng Chen, and Xing Xie. 2023. Defending chatgpt against jailbreak attack via self-reminder.

Penghao Wu and Saining Xie. 2024. V?: Guided visual search as a core mechanism in multimodal llms. In *Proceedings of the IEEE/CVF Conference on Computer Vision and Pattern Recognition*, pages 13084–13094.

Jiashu Xu, Mingyu Derek Ma, Fei Wang, Chaowei Xiao, and Muhao Chen. 2024a. Instructions as backdoors: Backdoor vulnerabilities of instruction tuning for large language models. In *NAACL*.

Nan Xu, Fei Wang, Ben Zhou, Bangzheng Li, Chaowei Xiao, and Muhao Chen. 2024b. Cognitive overload: Jailbreaking large language models with overloaded logical thinking. In *Findings of the Association for Computational Linguistics: NAACL 2024*, pages 3526–3548.

Rongwu Xu, Zehan Qi, Cunxiang Wang, Hongru Wang, Yue Zhang, and Wei Xu. 2024c. Knowledge conflicts for llms: A survey. *arXiv preprint arXiv:2403.08319*.

Fuzhao Xue, Zian Zheng, Yao Fu, Jinjie Ni, Zangwei Zheng, Wangchunshu Zhou, and Yang You. 2024. Openmoe: An early effort on open mixture-of-experts language models. *arXiv preprint arXiv:2402.01739*.

Shunyu Yao, Jeffrey Zhao, Dian Yu, Nan Du, Izhak Shafran, Karthik Narasimhan, and Yuan Cao. 2022. React: Synergizing reasoning and acting in language models. *ArXiv*, abs/2210.03629.

Qinyuan Ye, Maxamed Axmed, Reid Pryzant, and Fereshte Khani. 2023. Prompt engineering a prompt engineer. *arXiv preprint arXiv:2311.05661*.

Mert Yuksekgonul, Federico Bianchi, Joseph Boen, Sheng Liu, Zhi Huang, Carlos Guestrin, and James Zou. 2024. Textgrad: Automatic" differentiation" via text. *arXiv preprint arXiv:2406.07496*.

Yunxiang Zhang, Muhammad Khalifa, Lajanugen Logeswaran, Moontae Lee, Honglak Lee, and Lu Wang. Merging generated and retrieved knowledge for open-domain qa. In *The 2023 Conference on Empirical Methods in Natural Language Processing*.

Zheng Zhao, Emilio Monti, Jens Lehmann, and Haytham Assem. 2024. Enhancing contextual understanding in large language models through contrastive decoding. In *Proceedings of the 2024 Conference of the North American Chapter of the Association for Computational Linguistics: Human Language Technologies (Volume 1: Long Papers)*, pages 4225–4237.

Ben Zhou, Hongming Zhang, Sihao Chen, Dian Yu, Hongwei Wang, Baolin Peng, Dan Roth, and Dong Yu. 2024a. Conceptual and unbiased reasoning in language models. *arXiv preprint arXiv:2404.00205*.

Wenxuan Zhou, Sheng Zhang, Yu Gu, Muhao Chen, and Hoifung Poon. 2024b. Universalner: Targeted distillation from large language models for open named entity recognition. In *The Twelfth International Conference on Learning Representations*.

Wenxuan Zhou, Sheng Zhang, Hoifung Poon, and Muhao Chen. 2023. Context-faithful prompting for large language models. *arXiv preprint arXiv:2303.11315*.

Xuekai Zhu, Biqing Qi, Kaiyan Zhang, Xinwei Long, Zhouhan Lin, and Bowen Zhou. 2024. Pad: Program-aided distillation can teach small models reasoning better than chain-of-thought fine-tuning. In *Proceedings of the 2024 Conference of the North American Chapter of the Association for Computational Linguistics: Human Language Technologies (Volume 1: Long Papers)*, pages 2571–2597.

A Appendix

A.1 Past Tutorials by the Instructors

The presenters of this tutorial have given the following tutorials at leading international conferences in the past.

- Wenpeng Yin:
  - EMNLP'23: Learning from Task Instructions.
  - KONVENS'23: Learning from Task Instructions.
  - ACL'23: Indirectly Supervised Natural Language Processing.
- Muhao Chen:
  - ACL'23: Indirectly Supervised Natural Language Processing.
  - NAACL'22: New Frontiers of Information Extraction.
  - ACL'21: Event-Centric Natural Language Processing.
  - AAAI'21: Event-Centric Natural Language Understanding.
  - KDD'21: From Tables to Knowledge: Recent Advances in Table Understanding.
  - AAAI'20: Recent Advances of Transferable Representation Learning.
- Rui Zhang:
  - NAACL'22: Contrastive Data and Learning for Natural Language Processing
- Ben Zhou:
  - ACL'23: Indirectly Supervised Natural Language Processing.
  - NAACL'22: New Frontiers of Information Extraction
- Dan Roth:
  - ACL'23: Indirectly Supervised Natural Language Processing.
  - NAACL'22: New Frontiers of Information Extraction.
  - ACL'21: Event-Centric Natural Language Processing.
  - AAAI'21: Event-Centric Natural Language Understanding.
  - ACL'20: Commonsense Reasoning for Natural Language Processing.
  - AAAI'20: Recent Advances of Transferable Representation Learning.
  - ACL'18: A tutorial on Multi-lingual Entity Discovery and Linking.
  - EACL'17: A tutorial on Integer Linear Programming Formulations in Natural Language Processing.
  - AAAI'16: A tutorial on Structured Prediction.
  - ACL'14: A tutorial on Wikification and Entity Linking.
  - AAAI'13: Information Trustworthiness.
  - COLING'12: A Tutorial on Temporal Information Extraction and Shallow Temporal Reasoning.
  - NAACL'12: A Tutorial on Constrained Conditional Models: Structured Predictions in NLP.
  - NAACL'10: A Tutorial on Integer Linear Programming Methods in NLP.
  - EACL'09: A Tutorial on Constrained Conditional Models.
  - ACL'07: A Tutorial on Textual Entailment.

A.2 Recommended Paper List

The following is a reading list that could help provide background knowledge to the audience before attending this tutorial:

- Yuntao Bai, Andy Jones, Kamal Ndousse, Amanda Askell, Anna Chen, Nova DasSarma, Dawn Drain, Stanislav Fort, Deep Ganguli, Tom Henighan, et al. 2022. Training a helpful and harmless assistant with reinforcement learning from human feedback. arXiv
- Xinyun Chen, Maxwell Lin, Nathanael Schärli, and Denny Zhou. 2023a. Teaching large language models to self-debug. ArXiv
- Zhoujun Cheng, Jungo Kasai, and Tao Yu. 2023. Batch prompting: Efficient inference with large language model apis. CoRR, abs/2301.08721
- Jacob Devlin, Ming-Wei Chang, Kenton Lee, and Kristina Toutanova. 2019. BERT: pre-training of deep bidirectional transformers for language understanding. In Proceedings of NAACL-HLT
- Zhibin Gou, Zhihong Shao, Yeyun Gong, Yelong Shen, Yujiu Yang, Nan Duan, and Weizhu Chen. 2023. CRITIC: large language models can self-correct with tool-interactive critiquing. CoRR, abs/2305.11738

- Hangfeng He, Hongming Zhang, and Dan Roth. 2022. Rethinking with retrieval: Faithful large language model inference. arXiv preprint arXiv:2301.00303
- Yujin Huang, Terry Yue Zhuo, Qiongkai Xu, Han Hu, Xingliang Yuan, and Chunyang Chen. 2023. Training-free lexical backdoor attacks on language models. In Proceedings of the ACM Web Conference 2023
- Haoran Li, Dadi Guo, Wei Fan, Mingshi Xu, and Yangqiu Song. 2023a. Multi-step jailbreak- ing privacy attacks on chatgpt. arXiv
- Prateek Yadav, Derek Tam, Leshem Choshen, Colin Raf- fel, and Mohit Bansal. 2023. Resolving interference when merging models. CoRR, abs/2306.01708
- Jian Xie, Kai Zhang, Jiangjie Chen, Renze Lou, and Yu Su. 2023. Adaptive chameleon or stubborn sloth: Unraveling the behavior of large language models in knowledge conflicts. arXiv preprint arXiv:2305.13300
- Yashar Talebirad and Amirhossein Nadiri. 2023. Multi- agent collaboration: Harnessing the power of intelli- gent LLM agents. CoRR, abs/2306.03314.

Countering Hateful and Offensive Speech Online - Open Challenges

Flor Miriam Plaza-del-Arco
Bocconi University, Italy
flor.plaza@unibocconi.it

Debora Nozza
Bocconi University, Italy
debora.nozza@unibocconi.it

Marco Guerini
FBK, Italy
guerini@fbk.eu

Jeffrey Sorensen
Jigsaw, USA
sorenj@google.com

Marcos Zampieri
George Mason University, USA
mzampier@gmu.edu

Abstract

In today's digital age, hate speech and offensive speech online pose a significant challenge to maintaining respectful and inclusive online environments. This tutorial aims to provide attendees with a comprehensive understanding of the field by delving into essential dimensions such as multilingualism, counter-narrative generation, a hands-on session with one of the most popular APIs for detecting hate speech, fairness, and ethics in AI, and the use of recent advanced approaches. In addition, the tutorial aims to foster collaboration and inspire participants to create safer online spaces by detecting and mitigating hate speech.

1 Description

Hate Speech (HS) refers to any form of communication that belittles or targets individuals or groups based on characteristics such as race, color, ethnicity, gender, sexual orientation, nationality, religion, or other defining features.[1] This problem has experienced a rapid surge on the Web, especially on social media platforms, and contributes to the perpetuation of discrimination, division, and hostility in our society. Consequently, the need to identify and combat this issue has become increasingly imperative.

Automatic countering of HS and offensive language in Natural Language Processing (NLP) have experienced a surge in popularity since the 2010s, leading to the emergence of diverse resources and tasks within the community (Fersini et al., 2018; Basile et al., 2019; Plaza-del-Arco et al., 2021; Kirk et al., 2023). These range from conventional machine learning techniques using classifiers such as Support Vector Machines and Logistic Regression, to classification models based on the Transformer architecture, such as BERT or RoBERTa (Poletto et al., 2021; Fortuna et al., 2022). More recently, large language models (LLMs) have emerged as a promising alternative to address the challenges of supervised learning, using strategies like zero-shot and few-shot learning via prompting (Plaza-del-Arco et al., 2023).

HS countering faces considerable obstacles, particularly when dealing with languages or contexts that lack sufficient labeled data (Schmidt and Wiegand, 2017; Fortuna and Nunes, 2018). Additionally, HS is a subjective and context-dependent phenomenon, shaped by factors like demographics, social norms, cultural backgrounds (Waseem and Hovy, 2016; Ousidhoum et al., 2019). As a result, addressing this subjectivity has become a growing focus of research, with increasing attention given to incorporating multilingualism in the development of models and resources for detecting hate speech (Zampieri et al., 2020) and considering different vantage points (Weerasooriya et al., 2023).

While recent advancements in language models have demonstrated remarkable abilities in detecting such content, there is also a concerning observation that these models tend to capture and perpetuate biases, for instance, harmful stereotypes (Dixon et al., 2018; Vaidya et al., 2020; Nozza et al., 2021, 2022; Attanasio et al., 2022).

This tutorial aims to provide participants with a comprehensive understanding of countering hate speech and offensive language in NLP by delving into essential dimensions, including multilingualism, counter-narrative generation, practical sessions with the popular Perspective API, fairness and ethics, and the role of recent advances approaches with LLMs.

2 Type of Tutorial

This tutorial aims to present introductory NLP research on hate speech detection. Specifically, it will cover fundamental concepts related to hate speech, dataset creation, methodologies, techniques, practical sessions, and ethical considerations.

[1] https://ec.europa.eu/commission/presscorner/detail/en/ip_22_7109

Proceedings of the 2024 Conference on Empirical Methods in Natural Language Processing: Tutorial Abstracts, pages 11–16
November 12–16, 2024. ©2024 Association for Computational Linguistics

3 Pre-requisites

This tutorial caters to a diverse audience: NLP researchers who are currently involved in NLP for social good or have a strong interest in how to address hate speech detection in textual data; industry practitioners working in social media, online platforms, content moderation, and related domains that would like to have a general vision about how to combat hate speech; students, academics, and organizations interested in gaining insights about NLP techniques for hate speech detection.[2]

4 Outline

The tutorial will be 3.5 hours, including a half-hour coffee break. Over the course of this tutorial, we will delve into five key components.

4.1 Introduction [10 min]

This section serves as a comprehensive starting point, laying out the background, motivations, and overall structure of the tutorial.

4.2 Data Creation and Multilingualism [35 min]

Systems for automatic detection of offensive and hateful speech are usually developed using labeled training data and their performance is dependent on the quality of the available datasets (Poletto et al., 2021; Vidgen and Derczynski, 2021). There are various factors that impact data quality such as the data collection methods, the phenomena represented, and the taxonomies and guidelines used for annotation (Davidson et al., 2017; Rosenthal et al., 2021).

The creation of annotated multilingual datasets is crucial for training models that can accurately identify offensive and hateful speech across different languages and cultures. This process involves addressing challenges such as the scarcity of labeled data in low-resource languages, the variability in linguistic structures, and cultural differences in the expression of harmful language. In addition, the development of multilingual and cross-lingual language has opened new avenues for research in NLP. Such models allow researchers to take advantage of existing resources (e.g. datasets) in English and other high-resource languages to improve performance on languages with less resources (Ranasinghe and Zampieri, 2020).

In this part of the tutorial, we will discuss best practices in data creation and strategies to improve performance on low-resource scenarios using cross-lingual models and domain adaptation methods. We will also discuss the challenges of working with datasets that were designed according to different problem definitions and annotation taxonomies.

4.3 Counter-narrative Generation [35 min]

Tackling online hatred using argumentation-based textual responses – called counter-narratives – is an emerging topic in NLP. In particular, the focus is on automatically generating counter-narratives to intervene in online discussions and to prevent hate content from further spreading. Still, on the one hand, there is a lack of sufficient quality data, i.e., counter messages written by experts. Developing reliable data creation methods, such as sourcing expert-written counter-narratives or leveraging community-driven efforts with rigorous quality control is essential to improving model performance. On the other hand, LLMs still suffer from hallucinations, biases, and tend to produce generic/repetitive responses if they are not properly fine-tuned. In this section, we present and discuss several methodologies to collect high-quality counter-narratives efficiently and then describe the best generation strategies/neural architectures that can be used for counter-narrative generation.

4.4 Hands-on Session (Perspective API) [25 min]

Google has a long history of using machine learning as part of its implementation of moderation systems, as have other platforms. Making these tools available to smaller platforms is one way of sharing knowledge. Jigsaw has facilitated this through a variety of engagements with researchers and industry, including building multiple competitive machine learning tasks, sharing of labeled data, and provisioning state-of-the-art models at no cost to both researchers and media companies.

We will cover the basics of how one can obtain access and use this service to score data against a variety of models, and then discuss how the models are built and their limitations. We will also focus on the questions of fitness-for-task, potential harms from bias, and the evolving landscape of moderation as a service and the role of technology.

[2] Note: This tutorial assumes a basic understanding of NLP concepts, but the content will be presented in a way that is accessible to both beginners and more experienced individuals in the field.

4.5 Fairness & Ethics [30 min]

Online hate speech is rapidly increasing, with consequences that can lead to dangerous criminal acts offline. Because of its verbal nature, various NLP approaches have been proposed to counteract it, including those based on recent LLMs. However, several studies have shown that fine-tuning these neural language models on hate speech detection results in severe *unintended bias*, i.e., perform better or worse for comments mentioning specific *identity terms* (such as *gay*, *Muslim*, or *woman*). A key factor in mitigating this bias lies in the creation of balanced, high-quality datasets that accurately represent diverse groups without reinforcing harmful stereotypes. In this tutorial, we will discuss the risks of using ready-to-use classifiers on real-world data and various datasets and methods for measuring and mitigating this type of bias. As we delve into these solutions, we will also recognize the open challenge of striking the delicate balance between effectively identifying hate speech and ensuring a fair and just online environment for all.

4.6 How to use recent LLMs? [25 min]

LLMs have led to innovative techniques like prompting that use zero-shot and few-shot learning paradigms without needing labeled data. Zero-shot learning revolutionizes the traditional learning paradigm by enabling models to perform tasks on classes or domains for which they have never been explicitly trained. Prompting guides the model to infer relevant patterns and cues. In this tutorial, we will explore how to use recent LLMs by delving into different prompting techniques within a zero-shot learning setup and examine their effectiveness when applied to languages with limited data. Additionally, we will analyze how the choice of prompts and models influences the accuracy of predictions in the hate speech detection task.

4.7 Q&A and Discussion [20 min]

We will collect questions during the talks via an online platform and hold two 10-minute Q&A sessions: one before the coffee break and another at the end.

5 Reading List

We recommend that attendees read the following works:

- Vidgen and Derczynski (2021). Directions in abusive language training data, a systematic review: Garbage in, garbage out. *PLOS ONE.*
- Schmidt and Wiegand (2017). A Survey on Hate Speech Detection using Natural Language Processing. *In Proceedings of the Fifth International Workshop on Natural Language Processing for Social Media.*
- Zampieri et al. (2019). Predicting the Type and Target of Offensive Posts in Social Media. *In Proceedings of the 2019 Conference of the North American Chapter of the Association for Computational Linguistics: Human Language Technologies.*
- Tekiroğlu et al. (2020). Generating Counter Narratives against Online Hate Speech: Data and Strategies. *In Proceedings of the 58th Annual Meeting of the Association for Computational Linguistics.*
- Dixon et al. (2018) Measuring and Mitigating Unintended Bias in Text Classification. *In Proceedings of the 2018 AAAI/ACM Conference on AI, Ethics, and Society.*
- Plaza-del-Arco et al. (2023) Respectful or Toxic? Using Zero-Shot Learning with Language Models to Detect Hate Speech. *In Proceedings of the 7th Workshop on Online Abuse and Harms (WOAH).*

6 Instructors

Flor Miriam Plaza-del-Arco is a Postdoctoral Research Fellow at the MilaNLP group at Bocconi University. Her research focuses on leveraging NLP for social good, including hate speech detection, emotion analysis, biases in LLMs, and early risk prediction on the Web. During her Ph.D., she made significant contributions to hate speech detection, particularly in Spanish. She has also co-organized several events, including the eighth edition of the Workshop on Online Abuse and Harms (WOAH) and the EmoEvalEs and MeOffendES shared tasks at IberLef 2021.

Debora Nozza is an Assistant Professor in Computing Sciences at Bocconi University. Her research interests mainly focus on NLP, specifically on the detection and counter-acting of hate speech and algorithmic bias on Social Media data in multilingual context. She was one of the organizers of the task on Automatic Misogyny Identification (AMI) at Evalita 2018 and Evalita 2020, the Homotransphobia Detection in Italian (HODI) at Evalita 2023, and one of the organizers of the HatEval Task 5 at SemEval 2019 on multilingual detection of hate speech against immigrants and women in Twitter.

Marco Guerini is the head of the Language and Dialogue Technologies group at Fondazione Bruno Kessler (FBK). He works on NLP for persuasive communication, sentiment analysis and social media. In recent years his research has focused on the development of AI technologies to support counter narrative generation to fight online hate speech. He graduated in Philosophy and received his Ph.D. in Information and Communication Technologies from the University of Trento. He is author of several scientific publications in top-level conferences and international journals and organiser of workshops and share tasks.

Jeffrey Sorensen Jeffrey was part of the original team at Jigsaw that launched the Perspective API. Jeff joined Google in 2010 to work with the speech team, developing compact language models for use in on-device recognizer for mobile devices, and lead a team responsible for data collection and annotation. Jeffrey Sorensen has worked on machine learning models for speech recognition and translation, both for Google and previously for IBM.

Marcos Zampieri is an Assistant Professor at George Mason University in the United States. He has published papers on a variety topics in computational linguistics and NLP, including offensive language and hate speech identification. Marcos has co-organized multiple shared tasks at workshops such as BEA, SemEval, VarDial, and WMT. He has been the lead organizer of OffensEval-2019 and OffensEval-2020 at SemEval, two of the most popular offensive language identification tasks to date.

7 Diversity considerations

Our tutorial strongly values diversity as we focus on combating online abuse, hate, and related issues. Our diversity efforts include: 1) Inviting participation from various fields beyond NLP; 2) Reaching out to underrepresented NLP scholars; and 3) Forming a diverse organizing committee that embodies a wide range of backgrounds, experiences, and viewpoints, enriching the tutorial's guidance and impact.

8 Audience Size Estimation

Considering the historical attendance record of the related Workshop on Online Abuse and Harms (WOAH), coupled with the increasing societal and research focus on addressing online abuse, we anticipate a participation of 60-80 attendees.

9 Tutorial Materials

The tutorial materials are publicy available on GitHub.[3]

10 Ethics Statement

Our goal is to provide attendees with tools and knowledge to address these issues responsibly and enhance online safety. Throughout the tutorial, we will emphasize the importance of ethical considerations in hate speech detection and mitigation. We will explore not only the technical aspects but also the broader social and ethical implications of deploying hate speech detection systems. In addition, we are committed to promoting fairness, transparency, and accountability in the development and use of hate speech countering technologies. We will discuss the challenges posed by harmful biases and stereotypes in training data and the importance of identifying and mitigating these issues across the NLP models. Responsible and ethical approaches are essential to creating a positive impact in the field of hate speech countering.

Acknowledgments

Flor Miriam Plaza-del-Arco was supported by the European Research Council (ERC) under the European Union's Horizon 2020 research and innovation program (grant agreement No. 949944, INTEGRATOR). Debora Nozza was supported by the European Research Council (ERC) under the European Union's Horizon 2020 research and innovation program (grant agreement No. 101116095, PERSONAE). Flor Plaza and Debora Nozza are members of the MilaNLP group and the Data and Marketing Insights Unit of the Bocconi Institute for Data Science and Analysis (BIDSA). Marco Guerini was partially supported by the European Union's CERV fund under grant agreement No. 101143249 (HATEDEMICS). Marcos Zampieri was partially supported by the Virginia Commonwealth Cyber Initiative (CCI) award number N-4Q24-009.

[3]Countering Hateful and Offensive Speech Online - Open Challenges: `https://nlp-for-countering-hate-speech-tutorial.github.io/`.

References

Giuseppe Attanasio, Debora Nozza, Dirk Hovy, and Elena Baralis. 2022. Entropy-based attention regularization frees unintended bias mitigation from lists. In *Findings of the Association for Computational Linguistics: ACL 2022*, pages 1105–1119, Dublin, Ireland. Association for Computational Linguistics.

Valerio Basile, Cristina Bosco, Elisabetta Fersini, Debora Nozza, Viviana Patti, Francisco Manuel Rangel Pardo, Paolo Rosso, and Manuela Sanguinetti. 2019. SemEval-2019 task 5: Multilingual detection of hate speech against immigrants and women in Twitter. In *Proceedings of the 13th International Workshop on Semantic Evaluation*, pages 54–63, Minneapolis, Minnesota, USA. Association for Computational Linguistics.

Thomas Davidson, Dana Warmsley, Michael Macy, and Ingmar Weber. 2017. Automated hate speech detection and the problem of offensive language. In *Proceedings of the international AAAI conference on web and social media*, volume 11, pages 512–515.

Lucas Dixon, John Li, Jeffrey Sorensen, Nithum Thain, and Lucy Vasserman. 2018. Measuring and mitigating unintended bias in text classification. In *Proceedings of the 2018 AAAI/ACM Conference on AI, Ethics, and Society*, AIES '18, page 67–73, New York, NY, USA. Association for Computing Machinery.

Elisabetta Fersini, Debora Nozza, and Paolo Rosso. 2018. Overview of the Evalita 2018 Task on Automatic Misogyny Identification (AMI). In *EVALITA@CLiC-it*.

Paula Fortuna, Monica Dominguez, Leo Wanner, and Zeerak Talat. 2022. Directions for NLP practices applied to online hate speech detection. In *Proceedings of the 2022 Conference on Empirical Methods in Natural Language Processing*, pages 11794–11805, Abu Dhabi, United Arab Emirates. Association for Computational Linguistics.

Paula Fortuna and Sérgio Nunes. 2018. A survey on automatic detection of hate speech in text. *ACM Comput. Surv.*, 51(4).

Hannah Kirk, Wenjie Yin, Bertie Vidgen, and Paul Röttger. 2023. SemEval-2023 task 10: Explainable detection of online sexism. In *Proceedings of the The 17th International Workshop on Semantic Evaluation (SemEval-2023)*, pages 2193–2210, Toronto, Canada. Association for Computational Linguistics.

Debora Nozza, Federico Bianchi, and Dirk Hovy. 2021. HONEST: Measuring hurtful sentence completion in language models. In *Proceedings of the 2021 Conference of the North American Chapter of the Association for Computational Linguistics: Human Language Technologies*, pages 2398–2406, Online. Association for Computational Linguistics.

Debora Nozza, Federico Bianchi, Anne Lauscher, and Dirk Hovy. 2022. Measuring harmful sentence completion in language models for LGBTQIA+ individuals. In *Proceedings of the Second Workshop on Language Technology for Equality, Diversity and Inclusion*, pages 26–34, Dublin, Ireland. Association for Computational Linguistics.

Nedjma Ousidhoum, Zizheng Lin, Hongming Zhang, Yangqiu Song, and Dit-Yan Yeung. 2019. Multilingual and multi-aspect hate speech analysis. In *Proceedings of the 2019 Conference on Empirical Methods in Natural Language Processing and the 9th International Joint Conference on Natural Language Processing (EMNLP-IJCNLP)*, pages 4675–4684, Hong Kong, China. Association for Computational Linguistics.

Flor Miriam Plaza-del-Arco, Marco Casavantes, Hugo Jair Escalante, María Teresa Martín Valdivia, Arturo Montejo-Ráez, Manuel Montes-y-Gómez, Horacio Jesús Jarquín-Vásquez, and Luis Villaseñor Pineda. 2021. Overview of meoffendes at iberlef 2021: Offensive language detection in spanish variants. *Proces. del Leng. Natural*, 67:183–194.

Flor Miriam Plaza-del-Arco, Debora Nozza, and Dirk Hovy. 2023. Respectful or toxic? using zero-shot learning with language models to detect hate speech. In *The 7th Workshop on Online Abuse and Harms (WOAH)*, pages 60–68, Toronto, Canada. Association for Computational Linguistics.

Fabio Poletto, Valerio Basile, Manuela Sanguinetti, Cristina Bosco, and Viviana Patti. 2021. Resources and benchmark corpora for hate speech detection: a systematic review. *Language Resources and Evaluation*, 55:477–523.

Tharindu Ranasinghe and Marcos Zampieri. 2020. Multilingual offensive language identification with cross-lingual embeddings. In *Proceedings of the 2020 Conference on Empirical Methods in Natural Language Processing (EMNLP)*, pages 5838–5844.

Sara Rosenthal, Pepa Atanasova, Georgi Karadzhov, Marcos Zampieri, and Preslav Nakov. 2021. SOLID: A large-scale semi-supervised dataset for offensive language identification. In *Findings of the Association for Computational Linguistics: ACL-IJCNLP 2021*, pages 915–928, Online. Association for Computational Linguistics.

Anna Schmidt and Michael Wiegand. 2017. A survey on hate speech detection using natural language processing. In *Proceedings of the Fifth International Workshop on Natural Language Processing for Social Media*, pages 1–10, Valencia, Spain. Association for Computational Linguistics.

Serra Sinem Tekiroğlu, Yi-Ling Chung, and Marco Guerini. 2020. Generating counter narratives against online hate speech: Data and strategies. In *Proceedings of the 58th Annual Meeting of the Association for Computational Linguistics*, pages 1177–1190, Online. Association for Computational Linguistics.

Ameya Vaidya, Feng Mai, and Yue Ning. 2020. Empirical analysis of multi-task learning for reducing identity bias in toxic comment detection. In *Proceedings of the International AAAI Conference on Web and Social Media*, volume 14, pages 683–693.

Bertie Vidgen and Leon Derczynski. 2021. Directions in abusive language training data, a systematic review: Garbage in, garbage out. *PLOS ONE*, 15(12):1–32.

Zeerak Waseem and Dirk Hovy. 2016. Hateful symbols or hateful people? predictive features for hate speech detection on Twitter. In *Proceedings of the NAACL Student Research Workshop*, pages 88–93, San Diego, California. Association for Computational Linguistics.

Tharindu Weerasooriya, Sujan Dutta, Tharindu Ranasinghe, Marcos Zampieri, Christopher Homan, and Ashiqur KhudaBukhsh. 2023. Vicarious offense and noise audit of offensive speech classifiers: Unifying human and machine disagreement on what is offensive. In *Proceedings of the 2023 Conference on Empirical Methods in Natural Language Processing (EMNLP)*, pages 11648–11668.

Marcos Zampieri, Shervin Malmasi, Preslav Nakov, Sara Rosenthal, Noura Farra, and Ritesh Kumar. 2019. Predicting the type and target of offensive posts in social media. In *Proceedings of the 2019 Conference of the North American Chapter of the Association for Computational Linguistics: Human Language Technologies, Volume 1 (Long and Short Papers)*, pages 1415–1420, Minneapolis, Minnesota. Association for Computational Linguistics.

Marcos Zampieri, Preslav Nakov, Sara Rosenthal, Pepa Atanasova, Georgi Karadzhov, Hamdy Mubarak, Leon Derczynski, Zeses Pitenis, and Çağrı Çöltekin. 2020. SemEval-2020 task 12: Multilingual offensive language identification in social media (OffensEval 2020). In *Proceedings of the Fourteenth Workshop on Semantic Evaluation*, pages 1425–1447, Barcelona (online). International Committee for Computational Linguistics.

Language Agents: Foundations, Prospects, and Risks

Yu Su[1] **Diyi Yang**[2] **Shunyu Yao**[3] **Tao Yu**[4]
[1]The Ohio State University, [2]Stanford University, [3]Princeton University, [4]University of Hong Kong
su.809@osu.edu, diyiy@cs.stanford.edu, shunyuy@princeton.edu, tyu@cs.hku.hk

1 Introduction

A heated discussion thread in AI and NLP is *autonomous agents*, usually powered by large language models (LLMs), that can follow language instructions to carry out diverse and complex tasks in real-world or simulated environments. There are numerous proof-of-concept efforts on such agents recently, including ChatGPT Plugins,[1] AutoGPT,[2] generative agents (Park et al., 2023), just to name a few. The public is also showing an unprecedentedly high level of excitement. For example, AutoGPT has received 147K stars in just 4 months, making it the fastest growing repository in the Github history, despite its experimental nature with many known and sometimes serious limitations.

However, the concept of agent has been introduced into AI since its dawn. So what has changed recently? We argue that the most fundamental change is the capability of using language. Contemporary AI agents *use language as a vehicle for both thought and communication*, a trait that was unique to humans. This dramatically expands the breadth and depth of the problems these agents can possibly tackle, autonomously. The capability of using language, bestowed by their LLM foundations, allows these agents to 1) use a wide range of tools and reconcile their heterogeneous syntax and semantics (Parisi et al., 2022; Schick et al., 2023; Qin et al., 2023a; Patil et al., 2023; Qin et al., 2023b; Mialon et al., 2023), 2) operate in complex environments and ground to environment-specific semantics (Brohan et al., 2023b; Yao et al., 2022a; Gu et al., 2023; Wang et al., 2023a; Deng et al., 2023; Zhou et al., 2023), 3) conduct complex language-driven reasoning (Wei et al., 2022; Shinn et al., 2023; Chen et al., 2023), and 4) form spontaneous multi-agent systems (Park et al., 2023; Liu et al., 2023b). Therefore, to distinguish from the earlier AI agents, we suggest that these AI agents capable of using language for thought and communication should be called "*language agents*," for language being their most salient trait.

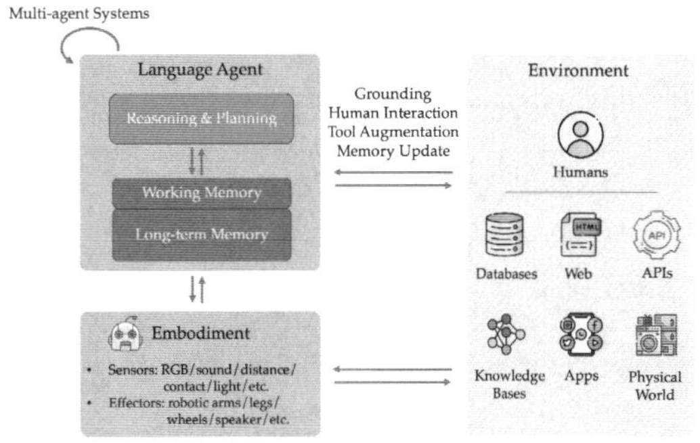

Figure 1: A conceptual framework for language agents.

Language played a critical role in the evolution of biological intelligence, and now artificial intelligence may be following a similar evolutionary path. This is remarkable and concerning at the same time. Despite the rapid progress, there has been a significant lack of systematic discussions regarding the conceptual definition, theoretical foundation, promising directions, and risks associated with language agents. This proposed tutorial endeavors to fill this gap by giving a comprehensive account of language agents based on both contemporary and classic AI research while drawing connections to cognitive science, neuroscience, and linguistics when appropriate.

2 Outline of Tutorial Content

This **cutting-edge** tutorial will be **half-day** and cover a conceptual framework for language agents as well as important topic areas including tool augmentation, grounding, reasoning and planning, multi-agent systems, and risks and societal impact.

2.1 Overview [30mins]

What are language agents and how they differ from the previous generations of AI agents? We

[1]https://openai.com/blog/chatgpt-plugins
[2]https://github.com/Significant-Gravitas/Auto-GPT

Proceedings of the 2024 Conference on Empirical Methods in Natural Language Processing: Tutorial Abstracts, pages 17–24
November 12–16, 2024.

will start by discussing why the capability of using language for thought and communication empowered by LLMs is the defining trait of the contemporary agents, drawing connections to the role language played in the evolution of biological intelligence (Dennett, 2013). We will then discuss a potential conceptual framework for language agents (Figure 1) and how each component (agent/embodiment/environment) differs from previous agents. One foundational construct is *memory*. We will discuss the resemblances and differences between a language agent/LLM's memory and human memory, including the storage mechanism (Kandel, 2007), long-term memory (LLM's parametric memory/vector databases), and working memory (in-context learning), and how such memory may support general-purpose language-driven reasoning. We will wrap up this section by outlining the key technical and societal aspects that will be discussed in the rest of the tutorial.

2.2 Tool Augmentation [30mins]

Tool augmentation or tool use (Schick et al., 2023; Mialon et al., 2023) is a natural extension of language agents due to their capability of using language for thought and communication. Language agents start to demonstrate a possibility of autonomously understanding and reconciling the heterogeneous syntax and semantics (e.g., XML vs. JSON) of different tools (i.e., using language for communication), and orchestrating the tool execution results into a coherent reasoning process (i.e., using language for thought). At present, tool augmentation mainly serves three purposes:

- Provide up-to-date and/or domain-specific information (Nakano et al., 2021; Lazaridou et al., 2022; Guu et al., 2020).
- Provide specialized capabilities (e.g., high-precision calculation) that a language agent may not have or be best at (Schick et al., 2023; Shen et al., 2023; Cheng et al., 2023; Gao et al., 2022).
- Enable a language agent to act in external environments (Liang et al., 2022; Wang et al., 2023a).

Two metrics are essential for practical tool augmentation: robustness, i.e., accuracy in using tools, and flexibility, i.e., ease of integrating a new tool. While existing efforts, e.g., ChatGPT Plugins, have made meaningful progress on flexibility, robustness still presents a significant challenge. This is particularly problematic for tools that produce side effects in the world (e.g., a tool for sending emails). We will discuss the challenges and opportunities around tool augmentation.

2.3 Grounding [30mins]

Most of the transformative applications of language agents involve connecting an agent to some real-world environments (e.g., through tools or embodiment), be it databases (Cheng et al., 2023), knowledge bases (Gu et al., 2023), the web (Deng et al., 2023; Zhou et al., 2023), or the physical world (Brohan et al., 2023a). Each environment is a unique context that provides possibly different interpretations of natural language. Grounding, i.e., the linking of (natural language) concepts to contexts (Chandu et al., 2021), thus becomes a central and pervasive challenge. There are two types of grounding related to language agents:

- Grounding natural language to an environment (Gu et al., 2023). This is also closely related to the *meaning* of natural language, which, as Bender and Koller (2020) put it, is the mapping from an utterance to its *communicative intent*.
- Grounding an agent's decisions in its own context (i.e., working memory), which includes external information from tools (Liu et al., 2023a; Yue et al., 2023; Gao et al., 2023; Cheng et al., 2023).

We will discuss the current work on both types of grounding, the remaining challenges, and promising future directions.

2.4 Reasoning and Planning [30mins]

The simplest way for language agents to interact with external worlds is to generate the next action via the LLM (Nakano et al., 2021; Schick et al., 2023), but the mapping from context to action is often non-trivial and such approaches often require fine-tuning to learn the mapping. Inspired by prior work that leverages intermediate reasoning to improve LLM performance (Nye et al., 2021; Wei et al., 2022), approaches such as ReAct (Yao et al., 2022b) start to leverage intermediate reasoning for better acting by flexibly analyzing environmental observations, making plans, tracking task status, recovering from exceptions, etc. Subsequent studies (Shinn et al., 2023; Chen et al., 2023) further leverage LLM reasoning for explicit self evaluation, critic, or reflection, to further improve agent performance. On the other hand, the simplest way for language agents to plan multiple steps of actions is to generate an action plan (Huang et al., 2022), but the token-by-token autoregressive decoding makes it hard to forecast planned future, backtrack from error, or maintain a global exploration structure for planning. To this end, recent works have begun to enhance LMs with re-planning (Song et al., 2022) or tree search algorithms (Yao et al., 2023; Hao et al., 2023) to systematically explore and make decisions in the planning space, analogous to planning-based agents such as AlphaGo (Silver et al., 2016). We will also discuss the recent trend that blurs the boundary between reasoning and acting, which leads to a more unified methodology between reasoning and planning (e.g., Monte-Carlo tree search applied for both reasoning (Hao et al., 2023) and action planning (Silver et al., 2016)).

2.5 Multi-Agent Systems [30mins]

When AI agents are equipped with the capability of using language for thought and communication, it starts to enable multi-agent systems quite different from the conventional ones (Ferber and Weiss, 1999)—agents can now act and communicate with each other in a more autonomous fashion. On the one hand, agents may now be generated with minimal specification instead of preprogrammed and can continually evolve through use and communication to produce complex social behaviors (Park et al., 2023), collaborate for task solving (Wu et al., 2023; Qian et al., 2023; Hong et al., 2023), or debate for more divergent and faithful reasoning (Chan et al., 2023; Liang et al., 2023; Du et al., 2023). On the other hand, human users are also agents, and these artificial language agents can interact with human agents in much richer and more flexible ways than before. There are numerous emerging opportunities, such as providing guardrails and alignment for language agents (Bai et al., 2022) and resolving uncertainties (Yao et al., 2020). We will discuss the opportunities and challenges in this new generation of multi-agent and human-AI collaborative systems.

2.6 Risks and Societal Impact [30mins]

Despite being powerful in a wide range of tasks, language agents are very likely to suffer from key risks and societal harms (Wang et al., 2023b). The first aspect is towards hallucination. The aforementioned memory module, retrieval, or even tool augmentation can largely increase faithfulness of model output, but hallucination issues might still exist and could lead to misleading, unsecure, and even harmful output especially when it comes to high-stake scenarios, raising key concerns towards privacy and truthfulness of the resulting interaction. Bias and fairness remain another primary risk, as language agents might inherit biases from the training corpus. The simulated AI agents might perpetuate stereotypes or discriminate against certain groups of people (Schramowski et al., 2022). Other potential risks include: the lack of transparency in why AI agents behave in their decision-making process, the robustness in AI agents in terms of being manipulated by malicious actors (Zou et al., 2023), and the ethics in terms of what AI agents can and cannot do, etc. Our tutorial will provide a detailed walkthrough of these potential risks in AI agents (Aher et al., 2023), using a few representative case studies to demonstrate how such risks might affect downstream applications, and how human-in-the-loop (Wu et al., 2022) or mixed initiative agents can be leveraged to build more responsible language agents. More importantly, we will briefly discuss the multifaceted impact of language agents, when it comes to user trust (Hancock et al., 2020; Liu et al., 2022), and cultural and societal implications. We will also discuss efforts on evaluating and benchmarking language agents (Liu et al., 2023c,d).

3 Other Required Information

The proposed tutorial is considered a **cutting-edge** tutorial that gives a systematic account of the emerging topic of language agents. There is no prior tutorial at *CL conferences that has covered this topic. There are a few recent tutorials *covering some related aspects* of language agents, such as "ACL'23: Tutorial on Complex Reasoning over Natural Language" on reasoning, "ACL'23: Retrieval-based Language Models and Applications" on retrieval augmentation, and "EMNLP'23: Mitigating Societal Harms in Large Language Models" on societal considerations of LLMs. However, there lacks a comprehensive coverage on the foundations, prospects, and risks of language agents, a void this proposed tutorial aspires to fill.

3.1 Target Audience and Prerequisites

This tutorial is targeted at a broad audience who are interested in language agents. There are no strict prerequisites for the audience's background, but having 1) basic knowledge of machine learning and deep learning and 2) basic knowledge of language models will help deeper understanding.

3.2 Diversity and Inclusion

We deeply value diversity and strongly believe it can greatly help realize the tutorial's goal and will ensure diversity in the following aspects:

Diversity of instructors. The instructor team has a diverse background including faculty members and graduate students from four institutes spanning two continents and from different gender groups.

Diversity of participants. Language agents are an emerging multi-disciplinary research topic with a very high level of interests in both academia and industry, so we expect a diverse audience. To further promote the awareness of the tutorial in underrepresented communities, we will work with affinity groups such as Black in AI, WiNLP, and LatinX in AI to broadcast the tutorial as well as solicit suggestions on the tutorial content.

Diversity of topics. Given the multi-disciplinary nature of language agents, the materials of this tutorial will cover both contemporary and classic AI/NLP research as well as related discussions from reinforcement learning, cognitive science, neuroscience, linguistics, human-computer interaction, and social science.

3.3 Tutorial Logistics

Estimated audience size. Based on prior tutorials and workshops we organized on related topics, we expect **100-150 attendees** including researchers and practitioners in related fields.

Open access. All materials will be released online on a dedicated website for the tutorial.

Preferred venue. We prefer to have the tutorial co-located with **ACL 2024** or **EMNLP 2024**.

3.4 Breadth

At least 60% of the tutorial will center around work done by researchers other than the instructors. This tutorial categorizes promising approaches for language agents into several groups, and each of these groups includes a significant amount of other researchers' works.

4 Tutorial Instructors

Yu Su is a distinguished assistant professor of engineering at the Ohio State University. His research investigates the role of language as a vehicle for thought and communication in artificial intelligence. His work at Microsoft has been deployed as the official conversational interface for Microsoft Outlook. His work on language agents has won awards such as Outstanding Paper Award at ACL'23 and COLING'22 and from the Amazon Alexa Prize Challenge. He has given 30+ invited talks internationally. Homepage: `https://ysu1989.github.io/`.

Diyi Yang is an assistant professor in the Computer Science Department at Stanford University. Her research focuses on human-centered natural language processing and computational social science. Diyi has organized four workshops at NLP conferences: Widening NLP Workshops at NAACL 2018 and ACL 2019, Causal Inference workshop at EMNLP 2021, NLG Evaluation workshop at EMNLP 2021, and Shared Stories and Lessons Learned workshop at EMNLP 2022. She gave a tutorial at ACL 2022 on Learning with Limited Data, and a tutorial at EACL 2023 on Summarizing Conversations at Scale. Homepage: `https://cs.stanford.edu/~diyiy/`.

Shunyu Yao is a PhD student at Princeton NLP Group, advised by Karthik Narasimhan and supported by Harold W. Dodds Fellowship. His research focuses on various facets of developing language agents, such as reasoning, acting, learning, and benchmarking. Homepage: `https://ysymyth.github.io`.

Tao Yu is an assistant professor of computer science at The University of Hong Kong. He completed his Ph.D. at Yale University and was a postdoctoral fellow at the University of Washington. His research aims to build language model agents that ground language instructions into code or actions executable in real-world environments. Tao is the recipient of an Amazon Research Award and Google Scholar Research Award. He has co-organized multiple workshops and a tutorial related to language agents at ACL, EMNLP, and NAACL. Homepage: `https://taoyds.github.io/`.

5 Ethics Statement

Language agents, with the ability of autonomously acting in the real world, pose significant potential ethical and safety risks. A main purpose of this proposed tutorial is to systematically define and analyze the unique capabilities and associated risks of language agents. We have a dedicated section on risks and societal impact, and we also cover related discussion in every other section when appropriate.

References

Gati V Aher, Rosa I Arriaga, and Adam Tauman Kalai. 2023. Using large language models to simulate multiple humans and replicate human subject studies. In *International Conference on Machine Learning*, pages 337–371. PMLR.

Yuntao Bai, Saurav Kadavath, Sandipan Kundu, Amanda Askell, Jackson Kernion, Andy Jones, Anna Chen, Anna Goldie, Azalia Mirhoseini, Cameron McKinnon, et al. 2022. Constitutional ai: Harmlessness from ai feedback. *arXiv preprint arXiv:2212.08073*.

Emily M. Bender and Alexander Koller. 2020. Climbing towards NLU: On meaning, form, and understanding in the age of data. In *Proceedings of the 58th Annual Meeting of the Association for Computational Linguistics*, pages 5185–5198, Online. Association for Computational Linguistics.

Anthony Brohan, Noah Brown, Justice Carbajal, Yevgen Chebotar, Xi Chen, Krzysztof Choromanski, Tianli Ding, Danny Driess, Avinava Dubey, Chelsea Finn, et al. 2023a. Rt-2: Vision-language-action models transfer web knowledge to robotic control. *arXiv preprint arXiv:2307.15818*.

Anthony Brohan, Yevgen Chebotar, Chelsea Finn, Karol Hausman, Alexander Herzog, Daniel Ho, Julian Ibarz, Alex Irpan, Eric Jang, Ryan Julian, et al. 2023b. Do as i can, not as i say: Grounding language in robotic affordances. In *Conference on Robot Learning*, pages 287–318. PMLR.

Chi-Min Chan, Weize Chen, Yusheng Su, Jianxuan Yu, Wei Xue, Shanghang Zhang, Jie Fu, and Zhiyuan Liu. 2023. Chateval: Towards better llm-based evaluators through multi-agent debate. *arXiv preprint arXiv:2308.07201*.

Khyathi Raghavi Chandu, Yonatan Bisk, and Alan W Black. 2021. Grounding 'grounding' in NLP. In *Findings of the Association for Computational Linguistics: ACL-IJCNLP 2021*, pages 4283–4305, Online. Association for Computational Linguistics.

Xinyun Chen, Maxwell Lin, Nathanael Schärli, and Denny Zhou. 2023. Teaching large language models to self-debug. *arXiv preprint arXiv:2304.05128*.

Zhoujun Cheng, Tianbao Xie, Peng Shi, Chengzu Li, Rahul Nadkarni, Yushi Hu, Caiming Xiong, Dragomir Radev, Mari Ostendorf, Luke Zettlemoyer, Noah A. Smith, and Tao Yu. 2023. Binding language models in symbolic languages. *ICLR*.

Xiang Deng, Yu Gu, Boyuan Zheng, Shijie Chen, Samuel Stevens, Boshi Wang, Huan Sun, and Yu Su. 2023. Mind2web: Towards a generalist agent for the web. *arXiv preprint arXiv:2306.06070*.

Daniel C Dennett. 2013. The role of language in intelligence. *Sprache und Denken/Language and Thought*, page 42.

Yilun Du, Shuang Li, Antonio Torralba, Joshua B Tenenbaum, and Igor Mordatch. 2023. Improving factuality and reasoning in language models through multiagent debate. *arXiv preprint arXiv:2305.14325*.

Jacques Ferber and Gerhard Weiss. 1999. *Multi-agent systems: an introduction to distributed artificial intelligence*, volume 1. Addison-wesley Reading.

Luyu Gao, Aman Madaan, Shuyan Zhou, Uri Alon, Pengfei Liu, Yiming Yang, Jamie Callan, and Graham Neubig. 2022. Pal: Program-aided language models. *ArXiv*, abs/2211.10435.

Tianyu Gao, Howard Yen, Jiatong Yu, and Danqi Chen. 2023. Enabling large language models to generate text with citations. *arXiv preprint arXiv:2305.14627*.

Yu Gu, Xiang Deng, and Yu Su. 2023. Don't generate, discriminate: A proposal for grounding language models to real-world environments. In *Proceedings of the 61st Annual Meeting of the Association for Computational Linguistics (Volume 1: Long Papers)*, pages 4928–4949, Toronto, Canada. Association for Computational Linguistics.

Kelvin Guu, Kenton Lee, Zora Tung, Panupong Pasupat, and Mingwei Chang. 2020. Retrieval augmented language model pre-training. In *International conference on machine learning*, pages 3929–3938. PMLR.

Jeffrey T Hancock, Mor Naaman, and Karen Levy. 2020. Ai-mediated communication: Definition, research agenda, and ethical considerations. *Journal of Computer-Mediated Communication*, 25(1):89–100.

Shibo Hao, Yi Gu, Haodi Ma, Joshua Jiahua Hong, Zhen Wang, Daisy Zhe Wang, and Zhiting Hu. 2023. Reasoning with language model is planning with world model. *arXiv preprint arXiv:2305.14992*.

Sirui Hong, Xiawu Zheng, Jonathan Chen, Yuheng Cheng, Ceyao Zhang, Zili Wang, Steven Ka Shing Yau, Zijuan Lin, Liyang Zhou, Chenyu Ran, et al. 2023. Metagpt: Meta programming for multi-agent collaborative framework. *arXiv preprint arXiv:2308.00352*.

Wenlong Huang, Pieter Abbeel, Deepak Pathak, and Igor Mordatch. 2022. Language models as zero-shot planners: Extracting actionable knowledge for embodied agents. In *International Conference on Machine Learning*, pages 9118–9147. PMLR.

Eric R Kandel. 2007. *In search of memory: The emergence of a new science of mind*. WW Norton & Company.

Angeliki Lazaridou, Elena Gribovskaya, Wojciech Stokowiec, and Nikolai Grigorev. 2022. Internet-augmented language models through few-shot prompting for open-domain question answering. *ArXiv*.

Jacky Liang, Wenlong Huang, F. Xia, Peng Xu, Karol Hausman, Brian Ichter, Peter R. Florence, and Andy Zeng. 2022. Code as policies: Language model programs for embodied control. *2023 IEEE International Conference on Robotics and Automation (ICRA)*, pages 9493–9500.

Tian Liang, Zhiwei He, Wenxiang Jiao, Xing Wang, Yan Wang, Rui Wang, Yujiu Yang, Zhaopeng Tu, and Shuming Shi. 2023. Encouraging divergent thinking in large language models through multi-agent debate. *arXiv preprint arXiv:2305.19118*.

Nelson F Liu, Tianyi Zhang, and Percy Liang. 2023a. Evaluating verifiability in generative search engines. *arXiv preprint arXiv:2304.09848*.

Ruibo Liu, Ruixin Yang, Chenyan Jia, Ge Zhang, Denny Zhou, Andrew M Dai, Diyi Yang, and Soroush Vosoughi. 2023b. Training socially aligned language models in simulated human society. *arXiv preprint arXiv:2305.16960*.

Xiao Liu, Hao Yu, Hanchen Zhang, Yifan Xu, Xuanyu Lei, Hanyu Lai, Yu Gu, Hangliang Ding, Kaiwen Men, Kejuan Yang, et al. 2023c. Agentbench: Evaluating llms as agents. *arXiv preprint arXiv:2308.03688*.

Yihe Liu, Anushk Mittal, Diyi Yang, and Amy Bruckman. 2022. Will ai console me when i lose my pet? understanding perceptions of ai-mediated email writing. In *Proceedings of the 2022 CHI conference on human factors in computing systems*, pages 1–13.

Zhiwei Liu, Weiran Yao, Jianguo Zhang, Le Xue, Shelby Heinecke, Rithesh Murthy, Yihao Feng, Zeyuan Chen, Juan Carlos Niebles, Devansh Arpit, et al. 2023d. Bolaa: Benchmarking and orchestrating llm-augmented autonomous agents. *arXiv preprint arXiv:2308.05960*.

Grégoire Mialon, Roberto Dessì, Maria Lomeli, Christoforos Nalmpantis, Ram Pasunuru, Roberta Raileanu, Baptiste Rozière, Timo Schick, Jane Dwivedi-Yu, Asli Celikyilmaz, et al. 2023. Augmented language models: a survey. *arXiv preprint arXiv:2302.07842*.

Reiichiro Nakano, Jacob Hilton, Suchir Balaji, Jeff Wu, Long Ouyang, Christina Kim, Christopher Hesse, Shantanu Jain, Vineet Kosaraju, William Saunders, et al. 2021. WebGPT: Browser-Assisted Question-Answering with Human Feedback. *arXiv preprint arXiv:2112.09332*.

Maxwell Nye, Anders Johan Andreassen, Guy Gur-Ari, Henryk Michalewski, Jacob Austin, David Bieber, David Dohan, Aitor Lewkowycz, Maarten Bosma, David Luan, et al. 2021. Show your work: Scratchpads for intermediate computation with language models. *arXiv preprint arXiv:2112.00114*.

Aaron Parisi, Yao Zhao, and Noah Fiedel. 2022. Talm: Tool augmented language models. *ArXiv*, abs/2205.12255.

Joon Sung Park, Joseph C O'Brien, Carrie J Cai, Meredith Ringel Morris, Percy Liang, and Michael S Bernstein. 2023. Generative agents: Interactive simulacra of human behavior. *arXiv preprint arXiv:2304.03442*.

Shishir G Patil, Tianjun Zhang, Xin Wang, and Joseph E Gonzalez. 2023. Gorilla: Large language model connected with massive apis. *arXiv preprint arXiv:2305.15334*.

Chen Qian, Xin Cong, Cheng Yang, Weize Chen, Yusheng Su, Juyuan Xu, Zhiyuan Liu, and Maosong Sun. 2023. Communicative agents for software development. *arXiv preprint arXiv:2307.07924*.

Yujia Qin, Shengding Hu, Yankai Lin, Weize Chen, Ning Ding, Ganqu Cui, Zheni Zeng, Yufei Huang, Chaojun Xiao, Chi Han, et al. 2023a. Tool learning with foundation models. *arXiv preprint arXiv:2304.08354*.

Yujia Qin, Shihao Liang, Yining Ye, Kunlun Zhu, Lan Yan, Yaxi Lu, Yankai Lin, Xin Cong, Xiangru Tang, Bill Qian, et al. 2023b. Toolllm: Facilitating large language models to master 16000+ real-world apis. *arXiv preprint arXiv:2307.16789*.

Timo Schick, Jane Dwivedi-Yu, Roberto Dessì, Roberta Raileanu, Maria Lomeli, Luke Zettlemoyer, Nicola Cancedda, and Thomas Scialom. 2023. Toolformer: Language models can teach themselves to use tools. *arXiv preprint arXiv:2302.04761*.

Patrick Schramowski, Cigdem Turan, Nico Andersen, Constantin A Rothkopf, and Kristian Kersting. 2022. Large pre-trained language models contain humanlike biases of what is right and wrong to do. *Nature Machine Intelligence*, 4(3):258–268.

Yongliang Shen, Kaitao Song, Xu Tan, Dong Sheng Li, Weiming Lu, and Yue Ting Zhuang. 2023. Hugginggpt: Solving ai tasks with chatgpt and its friends in hugging face. *ArXiv*, abs/2303.17580.

Noah Shinn, Federico Cassano, Beck Labash, Ashwin Gopinath, Karthik Narasimhan, and Shunyu Yao. 2023. Reflexion: Language agents with verbal reinforcement learning. *arXiv preprint arXiv:2303.11366*.

David Silver, Aja Huang, Chris J Maddison, Arthur Guez, Laurent Sifre, George Van Den Driessche, Julian Schrittwieser, Ioannis Antonoglou, Veda Panneershelvam, Marc Lanctot, et al. 2016. Mastering the game of go with deep neural networks and tree search. *nature*, 529(7587):484–489.

Chan Hee Song, Jiaman Wu, Clayton Washington, Brian M Sadler, Wei-Lun Chao, and Yu Su. 2022. Llm-planner: Few-shot grounded planning for embodied agents with large language models. *arXiv preprint arXiv:2212.04088*.

Guanzhi Wang, Yuqi Xie, Yunfan Jiang, Ajay Mandlekar, Chaowei Xiao, Yuke Zhu, Linxi Fan, and Anima Anandkumar. 2023a. Voyager: An open-ended embodied agent with large language models. *arXiv preprint arXiv:2305.16291*.

Lei Wang, Chen Ma, Xueyang Feng, Zeyu Zhang, Hao Yang, Jingsen Zhang, Zhiyuan Chen, Jiakai Tang, Xu Chen, Yankai Lin, et al. 2023b. A survey on large language model based autonomous agents. *arXiv preprint arXiv:2308.11432*.

Jason Wei, Xuezhi Wang, Dale Schuurmans, Maarten Bosma, Ed Chi, Quoc Le, and Denny Zhou. 2022. Chain of thought prompting elicits reasoning in large language models. *arXiv preprint arXiv:2201.11903*.

Qingyun Wu, Gagan Bansal, Jieyu Zhang, Yiran Wu, Shaokun Zhang, Erkang Zhu, Beibin Li, Li Jiang, Xiaoyun Zhang, and Chi Wang. 2023. Autogen: Enabling next-gen llm applications via multi-agent conversation framework. *arXiv preprint arXiv:2308.08155*.

Xingjiao Wu, Luwei Xiao, Yixuan Sun, Junhang Zhang, Tianlong Ma, and Liang He. 2022. A survey of human-in-the-loop for machine learning. *Future Generation Computer Systems*, 135:364–381.

Shunyu Yao, Howard Chen, John Yang, and Karthik Narasimhan. 2022a. Webshop: Towards scalable real-world web interaction with grounded language agents. *Advances in Neural Information Processing Systems*, 35:20744–20757.

Shunyu Yao, Dian Yu, Jeffrey Zhao, Izhak Shafran, Thomas L Griffiths, Yuan Cao, and Karthik Narasimhan. 2023. Tree of thoughts: Deliberate problem solving with large language models. *arXiv preprint arXiv:2305.10601*.

Shunyu Yao, Jeffrey Zhao, Dian Yu, Nan Du, Izhak Shafran, Karthik Narasimhan, and Yuan Cao. 2022b. React: Synergizing reasoning and acting in language models. *arXiv preprint arXiv:2210.03629*.

Ziyu Yao, Yiqi Tang, Wen-tau Yih, Huan Sun, and Yu Su. 2020. An imitation game for learning semantic parsers from user interaction. In *Proceedings of the 2020 Conference on Empirical Methods in Natural Language Processing (EMNLP)*, pages 6883–6902, Online. Association for Computational Linguistics.

Xiang Yue, Boshi Wang, Kai Zhang, Ziru Chen, Yu Su, and Huan Sun. 2023. Automatic evaluation of attribution by large language models. *arXiv preprint arXiv:2305.06311*.

Shuyan Zhou, Frank F Xu, Hao Zhu, Xuhui Zhou, Robert Lo, Abishek Sridhar, Xianyi Cheng, Yonatan Bisk, Daniel Fried, Uri Alon, et al. 2023. Webarena: A realistic web environment for building autonomous agents. *arXiv preprint arXiv:2307.13854*.

Andy Zou, Zifan Wang, J Zico Kolter, and Matt Fredrikson. 2023. Universal and transferable adversarial attacks on aligned language models. *arXiv preprint arXiv:2307.15043*.

Appendix

A Past Tutorials/Workshops by the Instructors

The instructors of the proposed tutorial have given tutorials or co-organized workshops at leading international conferences as follows:
Yu Su:

- ACL'21: Workshop on Natural Language Processing for Programming
- ACL'20: Workshop on Natural Language Interfaces
- WWW'18: Tutorial on Scalable Construction and Querying of Massive Knowledge Bases
- CIKM'17: Tutorial on Construction and Querying of Large-scale Knowledge Bases

Diyi Yang:

- EACL'23: Tutorial on Summarizing Conversations at Scale
- ACL'22: Tutorial on Learning with Limited Data
- EMNLP'21: Workshop on Causal Inference & NLP
- NAACL'18 & ACL'19: Widening NLP Workshop

Tao Yu:

- ACL'23: Tutorial on Complex Reasoning over Natural Language
- NAACL'22: Structured and Unstructured Knowledge Integration Workshop
- EMNLP'20: Interactive and Executable Semantic Parsing Workshop

B Recommended Reading List

The audience is recommended (but not required) to read the following papers before the tutorial to facilitate more engagement during the tutorial:

- Daniel C Dennett. The role of language in intelligence. (Dennett, 2013)

- Timo Schick, Jane Dwivedi-Yu, Roberto Dessì, Roberta Raileanu, Maria Lomeli, Luke Zettlemoyer, Nicola Cancedda, and Thomas Scialom. Toolformer: Language models can teach themselves to use tools. (Schick et al., 2023)

- Jason Wei, Xuezhi Wang, Dale Schuurmans, Maarten Bosma, Ed Chi, Quoc Le, and Denny Zhou. Chain of thought prompting elicits reasoning in large language models. (Wei et al., 2022)

- Shunyu Yao, Jeffrey Zhao, Dian Yu, Nan Du, Izhak Shafran, Karthik Narasimhan, and Yuan Cao. React: Synergizing reasoning and acting in language models. (Yao et al., 2022b)

- Gati V Aher, Rosa I Arriaga, and Adam Tauman Kalai. Using large language models to simulate multiple humans and replicate human subject studies. (Aher et al., 2023)

- Lei Wang, Chen Ma, Xueyang Feng, Zeyu Zhang, Hao Yang, Jingsen Zhang, Zhiyuan Chen, Jiakai Tang, Xu Chen, Yankai Lin, et al. A survey on large language model based autonomous agents. (Wang et al., 2023b)

- Yu Gu, Xiang Deng, and Yu Su. Don't generate, discriminate: A proposal for grounding language models to real-world environments. (Gu et al., 2023)

- Zhoujun Cheng, Tianbao Xie, Peng Shi, Chengzu Li, Rahul Nadkarni, Yushi Hu, Caiming Xiong, Dragomir Radev, Mari Ostendorf, Luke Zettlemoyer, Noah A. Smith, and Tao Yu. Binding language models in symbolic languages. (Cheng et al., 2023)

- Joon Sung Park, Joseph C O'Brien, Carrie J Cai, Meredith Ringel Morris, Percy Liang, and Michael S Bernstein. Generative agents: Interactive simulacra of human behavior. (Park et al., 2023)

- Patrick Schramowski, Cigdem Turan, Nico Andersen, Constantin A Rothkopf, and Kristian Kersting. Large pre-trained language models contain human-like biases of what is right and wrong to do. (Schramowski et al., 2022)

- Emily M. Bender and Alexander Koller. Climbing towards NLU: On meaning, form, and understanding in the age of data. (Bender and Koller, 2020)

Reasoning with Natural Language Explanations

Marco Valentino[1], **André Freitas**[1,2,3]
[1]Idiap Research Institute, Switzerland,
[2]Department of Computer Science, University of Manchester, UK
[3]National Biomarker Centre, CRUK-MI, University of Manchester, UK
first.last@idiap.ch

Abstract

Explanation constitutes an archetypal feature of human rationality, underpinning learning, and generalisation, and representing one of the media supporting scientific discovery and communication. Due to the importance of explanations in human reasoning, an increasing amount of research in Natural Language Inference (NLI) has started reconsidering the role that explanations play in learning and inference, attempting to build explanation-based NLI models that can effectively encode and use natural language explanations on downstream tasks. Research in explanation-based NLI, however, presents specific challenges and opportunities, as explanatory reasoning reflect aspects of both material and formal inference, making it a particularly rich setting to model and deliver complex reasoning. In this tutorial, we provide a comprehensive introduction to the field of explanation-based NLI, grounding this discussion on the epistemological-linguistic foundations of explanations, systematically describing the main architectural trends and evaluation methodologies which can be used to build systems which are capable of explanatory reasoning[1].

1 Introduction

Building systems that can understand and explain the world is a long-standing goal for *Artificial Intelligence (AI)* (Miller, 2019; Mitchell et al., 1986; Thagard and Litt, 2008). The ability to explain, in fact, constitutes an archetypal feature of human rationality, underpinning communication, learning, and generalisation, as well as one of the mediums enabling scientific discovery and progress through the formulation of explanatory theories (Lombrozo, 2012; Salmon, 2006; Kitcher, 1989; Deutsch, 2011).

Due to the importance of explanation in human reasoning, an increasing amount of work has started reconsidering the role that explanation plays in learning and inference with natural language (Camburu et al., 2018; Yang et al., 2018; Rajani et al., 2019; Jansen et al., 2018). In contrast to the existing end-to-end paradigm based on Deep Learning, explanation-based NLI focuses on developing and evaluating models that can address downstream tasks through the explicit construction of a *natural language explanation* (Dalvi et al., 2021; Jansen et al., 2016; Wiegreffe and Marasović, 2021; Stacey et al., 2022). In this context, explanation is seen as a potential solution to mitigate some of the well-known limitations in neural-based NLI architectures (Thayaparan et al., 2020), including the susceptibility to learning via shortcuts, the inability to generalise out-of-distribution, and the lack of interpretability (Guidotti et al., 2018; Biran and Cotton, 2017; Geirhos et al., 2020; Lewis et al., 2021; Sinha et al., 2021; Schlegel et al., 2020).

Research in explanation-based NLI, however, presents several fundamental challenges (Valentino and Freitas, 2024). First, the applied methodologies are still poorly informed by theories and accounts of explanations (Salmon, 2006; Woodward and Ross, 2021). This gap between theory and practice poses the risk of slowing down progress, missing the opportunity to formulate clearer hypotheses on the inferential properties of natural language explanations and define systematic evaluation methodologies (Camburu et al., 2020; Jansen et al., 2021; Atanasova, 2024). Second, explanation-based NLI models still lack robustness, control, and scalability for real-world applications. In particular, existing approaches suffer from several limitations when composing explanatory reasoning chains and performing abstraction for NLI in complex domains (Khashabi et al., 2019; Valentino et al., 2022a).

In this tutorial, we will provide a comprehensive introduction to explanatory reasoning in the context of NLI, by systematically categorising and surveying explanation-supporting benchmarks, ar-

[1]Tutorial website: https://sites.google.com/view/reasoning-with-explanations

Proceedings of the 2024 Conference on Empirical Methods in Natural Language Processing: Tutorial Abstracts, pages 25–31
November 12-16, 2024.

chitectures, and research trends. Specifically, we will present how the understanding of explanatory inference have evolved in recent years, together with the emerging methodological and modelling strategies. In parallel, we will attempt to provide an epistemological-linguistic characterisation of natural language explanations reviewing the main theoretical accounts (Valentino and Freitas, 2024; Salmon, 2006) to derive a fresh perspective for future work in the field.

2 Description

This section outlines the content of the tutorial.

2.1 Epistemological-Linguistic Foundations

One of the main objectives of the tutorial is to provide a theoretically grounded foundation for explanation-based NLI, investigating the notion of explanation as a language and inference scientific object of interest, from both an *epistemological* and *linguistic* perspectives (Valentino and Freitas, 2024; Salmon, 2006; Jansen et al., 2016).

To this end, we will present a systematic survey of the contemporary discussion in Philosophy of Science around the notion of a scientific explanation, attempting to shed light on the nature and function of explanatory arguments and their constituting elements. Here, we will critically review the main accounts of explanations, including the deductive-nomological and inductive-statistical account (Hempel and Oppenheim, 1948), the notion of statistical relevance and the causal-mechanical model (Salmon, 1984), and the unificationist account (Kitcher, 1989), aiming to elicit what it means to perform explanatory reasoning. Following the survey, we will focus on grounding the theoretical accounts for explanation-based NLI, attempting to identify the main feature of explanatory arguments in existing corpora of natural language explanations (Jansen et al., 2016; Xie et al., 2020; Jansen et al., 2018).

2.2 Resources & Evaluation Methods for Explanation-Based NLI

In order to build NLI models that can reason through the generation of natural language explanations it is necessary to develop systematic evaluation methodologies. To this end, The tutorial will review the main resources, benchmarks and metrics in the field (Wiegreffe and Marasovic).

Depending on the nature of the NLI problem, an explanation can include pieces of evidence at different levels of abstraction (Thayaparan et al., 2020). Traditionally, the field has been divided into *extractive* and *abstractive* tasks. In extractive NLI, the reasoning required for the explanations is derivable from the original problem formulation, where the correct decomposition of the problem contains all the necessary inference steps for the answer (Yang et al., 2018). On the other hand, abstractive NLI tasks require going beyond the surface form of the problem, where an explanation needs to account for and cohere definitions, abstract relations, which are not immediately available from the original context (Jansen et al., 2021; Thayaparan et al., 2021b).

In addition, the tutorial will review the main evaluation metrics adopted to assess the quality of natural language explanations. Evaluating the quality of explanations, in fact, is a challenging problem as it requires accounting for multiple concurrent properties. Different metrics have been proposed in the field, ranging from reference-based metrics designed to assess the alignment between automatically generated explanations and human-annotated explanations (Camburu et al., 2018; Jansen et al., 2021), and reference-free metrics designed to evaluate additional dimensions such as faithfulness (Parcalabescu and Frank, 2024; Atanasova et al., 2023), robustness (Camburu et al., 2020), logical validity (Quan et al., 2024b; Valentino et al., 2021a), and plausibility (Dalal et al., 2024).

2.3 Explanation-Based Learning & Inference

We review the key architectural patterns and modelling strategies for reasoning and learning over natural language explanations. In particular, we focus on the following paradigms:

Multi-Hop Reasoning & Retrieval-Based Models. The construction of explanations typically requires multi-hop reasoning – i.e., the ability to compose multiple pieces of evidence to support the final answer (Dalvi et al., 2021; Xie et al., 2020). Multi-hop reasoning has been largely studied in a retrieval settings, where, given an external knowledge base, the model is required to select, collect and link the relevant knowledge required to arrive at a final answer (Valentino et al., 2022a, 2021b, 2022b). Here, we will review the main retrieval-based architectures for multi-hop reasoning and explanation, highlighting some of the inherent limitations of such paradigm, including the tension between semantic drift and efficiency (Khashabi et al., 2019).

Natural Language Explanation Generation. In parallel with retrieval approaches, NLI using generative models have been used for supporting explanatory inference (Camburu et al., 2018; Rajani et al., 2019). In this setting, early approaches leverage human-annotated natural language explanations for training generative models (Dalvi et al., 2021). Subsequently, the advent of Large Language Models (LLMs) has made it possible to elicit explanatory reasoning via specific prompting techniques and in-context learning (Wei et al., 2022; Yao et al., 2024; Zheng et al., 2023; He et al., 2024). Here, we review the main trends in the LLM-based generative paradigms, highlighting persisting limitations such as hallucinations and faithfulness (Turpin et al., 2024).

2.4 Semantic Control for Explanatory Reasoning

Controlling the explanation generation process in neural-based models is particularly critical while modelling complex reasoning tasks. In this tutorial, we will review emerging trends which combine neural and symbolic approaches to improve semantic control in the explanatory reasoning process, which can provide formal guarantees on the quality of the explanations. These methods aim to integrate the content flexibility of language models (instrumental for supporting material inferences) and a formal inference properties.

In particular, we focus on the following key methods:

Leveraging Explanatory Inference Patterns for Explanation-Based NLI. Inference patterns in explanation corpora can be leveraged to improve the efficiency and robustness of neural representations (Valentino and Freitas, 2024; Zhang et al., 2023). In particular, we will review approaches that attempt to leverage the notion of unification power in corpora of natural language explanations to improve multi-hop reasoning in a retrieval setting and alleviate semantic drift (Valentino et al., 2022a, 2021b, 2022b).

Constraint-Based Optimisation for Explanation-Based NLI. We will focus on describing neuro-symbolic methods which target encoding explicit assumptions about the structure of natural language explanations (Thayaparan et al., 2021a). Here, we will review methods performing multi-hop inference via constrained optimisation, integrating neural representations with explicit constraints via end-to-end differentiable optimisation approaches (Thayaparan et al., 2022, 2024).

Formal-Geometric Inference Controls over Latent Spaces. Covers emerging methodologies which focus on learning latent spaces with better representational properties for explanatory NLI, using language Variational Autoencoders (VAEs) for delivering better disentanglement and separability of language and inference properties (Zhang et al., 2024a,c,b,a) which support better inference control. These methods deliver an additional geometrical structure to latent spaces, aiming to deliver the vision of 'inference as latent geometry'.

LLM-Symbolic Architectures Finally, we will focus on hybrid neuro-symbolic architectures that attempt to leverage the material/content-based inference properties of LLMs for explanation generation with external symbolic approaches, which accounts for formal/logical validity refinement properties. In particular, we will review approaches that perform explanation refinement via the integration of LLMs and Theorem Provers to verify logical validity (Quan et al., 2024b,a) and additional external tools to evaluate explanation properties such as uncertainty, plausibility and coherence (Dalal et al., 2024).

3 Schedule

The tutorial will be organised according to the following timeline:

1. Introduction & Motivation (20 min.)
2. Epistemological-Linguistic Foundations (20 min.)
3. Resources & Evaluation for Explanation-Based NLI (40 min.)
4. Explanation-Based Learning & Inference (40 min.)
5. Semantic Control for Explanatory Reasoning (40 min.)
6. Synthesis, Discussion, and Q&A (20 min)

4 Breadth & Diversity

The tutorial will cover a wide spectrum of topics in different fields, ranging from Philosophy,

Machine Learning, Natural Language Processing, Knowledge Representation and Automated Reasoning. This diversity of topics will help create a rich environment in which academics from different backgrounds and cultural contexts can integrate different perspectives. The tutorial plan includes integrated open Q&A sessions and practical demonstrations.

5 Prerequisites

We do not expect attendees to be familiar with previous research on NLI and Explanatory inference. On the opposite, we intent this tutorial to be an efficient and deep onboarding into the state-of-the-art in those areas. Participants should have a general background knowledge in deep learning, including recent trends and architectures such as Large Language Models. Participants are expected to be familiar with some of the broader NLI tasks, such as Textual Entailment and Question Answering.

6 Reading List

Epistemological-Linguistic Foundations

Valentino and Freitas (2024) On the Nature of Explanation: An Epistemological-Linguistic Perspective for Explanation-Based Natural Language Inference.

Salmon (2006) Four Decades of Scientific Explanation.

Jansen et al. (2016) What's in an Explanation? Characterizing Knowledge and Inference Requirements for Elementary Science Exam.

Resources, Models and Evaluation

Wiegreffe and Marasović (2021) Teach me to Explain: A Review of Datasets for Explainable Natural Language Processing.

Thayaparan et al. (2020) A Survey on Explainability in Machine Reading Comprehension.

Zhao et al. (2024) Explainability for Large Language Models: A Survey.

Related Tutorials

Zhu et al. (2024) Explanation in the Era of Large Language Models.

Camburu and Akata (2021) Natural-XAI: Explainable AI with Natural Language Explanation.

Zhao et al. (2023) Complex Reasoning in Natural Language.

Boyd-Graber et al. (2022) Human-Centered Evaluation of Explanations.

7 Instructor information

Marco Valentino, Idiap Research Institute.[2] Marco is a postdoctoral researcher at the Idiap Research Institute, Switzerland. His research is carried out at the intersection of Natural Language Inference and Neuro-Symbolic models focusing on building systems that can reason through natural language explanations in complex domains (e.g., mathematics, science, biomedical and clinical applications, ethical reasoning). He has published papers in major AI and NLP conferences including AAAI, ACL, EMNLP, NAACL and EACL. Marco was involved in the organisation of workshops including MathNLP (EMNLP 2022 and LREC-COLING 2024), and TextGraphs (COLING 2022 and ACL 2024).

André Freitas, University of Manchester & Idiap Research Institute.[3] André Freitas leads the Neuro-symbolic AI Lab at the University of Manchester and IDIAP Research Institute. His main research interests are on enabling the development of AI methods to support abstract, flexible and controlled reasoning in order to support AI-augmented scientific discovery. In particular, he investigates how the combination of neural and symbolic data representation paradigms can deliver better models of inference. He is an active contributor to the main conferences and journals in the AI/Natural Language Processing (NLP) interface (AAAI, NeurIPs, ACL, EMNLP, EACL, COLING, TACL, Computational Linguistics), with over 100 peer-reviewed publications. He contributed to the organisation of MathNLP at EMNLP 2022 and LREC-COLING 2024. André participated in 7 tutorials, and co-organised 1 conference and 6 workshops.

Acknowledgements

This work was partially funded by the Swiss National Science Foundation (SNSF) project NeuMath (200021_204617).

[2] mailto:marco.valentino@idiap.ch

[3] mailto:andre.freitas@manchester.ac.uk

References

P Atanasova, OM Camburu, C Lioma, T Lukasiewicz, JG Simonsen, and I Augenstein. 2023. Faithfulness tests for natural language explanations. In *Proceedings of the Annual Meeting of the Association for Computational Linguistics*, volume 2, pages 283–294. Association for Computational Linguistics (ACL).

Pepa Atanasova. 2024. A diagnostic study of explainability techniques for text classification. In *Accountable and Explainable Methods for Complex Reasoning over Text*, pages 155–187. Springer.

Or Biran and Courtenay Cotton. 2017. Explanation and justification in machine learning: A survey. In *IJCAI-17 workshop on explainable AI (XAI)*, volume 8.

Jordan Boyd-Graber, Samuel Carton, Shi Feng, Q. Vera Liao, Tania Lombrozo, Alison Smith-Renner, and Chenhao Tan. 2022. Human-centered evaluation of explanations. In *Proceedings of the 2022 Conference of the North American Chapter of the Association for Computational Linguistics: Human Language Technologies: Tutorial Abstracts*, pages 26–32, Seattle, United States. Association for Computational Linguistics.

Oana-Maria Camburu and Zeynep Akata. 2021. Natural-xai: Explainable ai with natural language explanations. In *International Conference on Machine Learning*.

Oana-Maria Camburu, Tim Rocktäschel, Thomas Lukasiewicz, and Phil Blunsom. 2018. e-snli: Natural language inference with natural language explanations. In *Advances in Neural Information Processing Systems*, pages 9539–9549.

Oana-Maria Camburu, Brendan Shillingford, Pasquale Minervini, Thomas Lukasiewicz, and Phil Blunsom. 2020. Make up your mind! adversarial generation of inconsistent natural language explanations. In *Proceedings of the 58th Annual Meeting of the Association for Computational Linguistics*, pages 4157–4165, Online. Association for Computational Linguistics.

Dhairya Dalal, Marco Valentino, Andre Freitas, and Paul Buitelaar. 2024. Inference to the best explanation in large language models. In *Proceedings of the 62nd Annual Meeting of the Association for Computational Linguistics (Volume 1: Long Papers)*, pages 217–235, Bangkok, Thailand. Association for Computational Linguistics.

Bhavana Dalvi, Peter Jansen, Oyvind Tafjord, Zhengnan Xie, Hannah Smith, Leighanna Pipatanangkura, and Peter Clark. 2021. Explaining answers with entailment trees. In *Proceedings of the 2021 Conference on Empirical Methods in Natural Language Processing*, pages 7358–7370.

David Deutsch. 2011. *The beginning of infinity: Explanations that transform the world.* Penguin UK.

Robert Geirhos, Jörn-Henrik Jacobsen, Claudio Michaelis, Richard Zemel, Wieland Brendel, Matthias Bethge, and Felix A Wichmann. 2020. Shortcut learning in deep neural networks. *Nature Machine Intelligence*, 2(11):665–673.

Riccardo Guidotti, Anna Monreale, Salvatore Ruggieri, Franco Turini, Fosca Giannotti, and Dino Pedreschi. 2018. A survey of methods for explaining black box models. *ACM computing surveys (CSUR)*, 51(5):1–42.

Xuanli He, Yuxiang Wu, Oana-Maria Camburu, Pasquale Minervini, and Pontus Stenetorp. 2024. Using natural language explanations to improve robustness of in-context learning. In *Proceedings of the 62nd Annual Meeting of the Association for Computational Linguistics (Volume 1: Long Papers)*, pages 13477–13499, Bangkok, Thailand. Association for Computational Linguistics.

Carl G Hempel and Paul Oppenheim. 1948. Studies in the logic of explanation. *Philosophy of science*, 15(2):135–175.

Peter Jansen, Niranjan Balasubramanian, Mihai Surdeanu, and Peter Clark. 2016. What's in an explanation? characterizing knowledge and inference requirements for elementary science exams. In *Proceedings of COLING 2016, the 26th International Conference on Computational Linguistics: Technical Papers*, pages 2956–2965.

Peter Jansen, Kelly J Smith, Dan Moreno, and Huitzilin Ortiz. 2021. On the challenges of evaluating compositional explanations in multi-hop inference: Relevance, completeness, and expert ratings. In *Proceedings of the 2021 Conference on Empirical Methods in Natural Language Processing*, pages 7529–7542.

Peter Jansen, Elizabeth Wainwright, Steven Marmorstein, and Clayton Morrison. 2018. Worldtree: A corpus of explanation graphs for elementary science questions supporting multi-hop inference. In *Proceedings of the Eleventh International Conference on Language Resources and Evaluation (LREC 2018).*

Daniel Khashabi, Erfan Sadeqi Azer, Tushar Khot, Ashish Sabharwal, and Dan Roth. 2019. On the capabilities and limitations of reasoning for natural language understanding. *arXiv preprint arXiv:1901.02522.*

Philip Kitcher. 1989. Explanatory unification and the causal structure of the world.

Patrick Lewis, Pontus Stenetorp, and Sebastian Riedel. 2021. Question and answer test-train overlap in open-domain question answering datasets. In *Proceedings of the 16th Conference of the European Chapter of the Association for Computational Linguistics: Main Volume*, pages 1000–1008.

Tania Lombrozo. 2012. Explanation and abductive inference. *Oxford handbook of thinking and reasoning*, pages 260–276.

Tim Miller. 2019. Explanation in artificial intelligence: Insights from the social sciences. *Artificial Intelligence*, 267:1–38.

Tom M Mitchell, Richard M Keller, and Smadar T Kedar-Cabelli. 1986. Explanation-based generalization: A unifying view. *Machine learning*, 1(1):47–80.

Letitia Parcalabescu and Anette Frank. 2024. On measuring faithfulness or self-consistency of natural language explanations. In *Proceedings of the 62nd Annual Meeting of the Association for Computational Linguistics (Volume 1: Long Papers)*, pages 6048–6089.

Xin Quan, Marco Valentino, Louise Dennis, and Andre Freitas. 2024a. Enhancing ethical explanations of large language models through iterative symbolic refinement. In *Proceedings of the 18th Conference of the European Chapter of the Association for Computational Linguistics (Volume 1: Long Papers)*, pages 1–22, St. Julian's, Malta. Association for Computational Linguistics.

Xin Quan, Marco Valentino, Louise A Dennis, and André Freitas. 2024b. Verification and refinement of natural language explanations through llm-symbolic theorem proving. *arXiv preprint arXiv:2405.01379*.

Nazneen Fatema Rajani, Bryan McCann, Caiming Xiong, and Richard Socher. 2019. Explain yourself! leveraging language models for commonsense reasoning. In *Proceedings of the 57th Annual Meeting of the Association for Computational Linguistics*, pages 4932–4942.

Wesley C Salmon. 1984. *Scientific explanation and the causal structure of the world*. Princeton University Press.

Wesley C Salmon. 2006. *Four decades of scientific explanation*. University of Pittsburgh press.

Viktor Schlegel, Marco Valentino, André Freitas, Goran Nenadic, and Riza Theresa Batista-Navarro. 2020. A framework for evaluation of machine reading comprehension gold standards. In *Proceedings of The 12th Language Resources and Evaluation Conference*, pages 5359–5369.

Koustuv Sinha, Prasanna Parthasarathi, Joelle Pineau, and Adina Williams. 2021. Unnatural language inference. In *Proceedings of the 59th Annual Meeting of the Association for Computational Linguistics and the 11th International Joint Conference on Natural Language Processing (Volume 1: Long Papers)*, pages 7329–7346.

Joe Stacey, Yonatan Belinkov, and Marek Rei. 2022. Supervising model attention with human explanations for robust natural language inference. In *Proceedings of the AAAI Conference on Artificial Intelligence*, volume 36, pages 11349–11357.

Paul Thagard and Abninder Litt. 2008. Models of scientific explanation. *The Cambridge Handbook of Computational Psychology*, pages 549–564.

Mokanarangan Thayaparan, Marco Valentino, Deborah Ferreira, Julia Rozanova, and André Freitas. 2022. Diff-explainer: Differentiable convex optimization for explainable multi-hop inference. *Transactions of the Association for Computational Linguistics*, 10:1103–1119.

Mokanarangan Thayaparan, Marco Valentino, and André Freitas. 2020. A survey on explainability in machine reading comprehension. *arXiv preprint arXiv:2010.00389*.

Mokanarangan Thayaparan, Marco Valentino, and André Freitas. 2021a. Explainable inference over grounding-abstract chains for science questions. In *Findings of the Association for Computational Linguistics: ACL-IJCNLP 2021*, pages 1–12.

Mokanarangan Thayaparan, Marco Valentino, and André Freitas. 2024. A differentiable integer linear programming solver for explanation-based natural language inference. In *Proceedings of the 2024 Joint International Conference on Computational Linguistics, Language Resources and Evaluation (LREC-COLING 2024)*, pages 449–458.

Mokanarangan Thayaparan, Marco Valentino, Peter Jansen, and Dmitry Ustalov. 2021b. TextGraphs 2021 shared task on multi-hop inference for explanation regeneration. In *Proceedings of the Fifteenth Workshop on Graph-Based Methods for Natural Language Processing (TextGraphs-15)*, pages 156–165, Mexico City, Mexico. Association for Computational Linguistics.

Miles Turpin, Julian Michael, Ethan Perez, and Samuel Bowman. 2024. Language models don't always say what they think: unfaithful explanations in chain-of-thought prompting. *Advances in Neural Information Processing Systems*, 36.

Marco Valentino and André Freitas. 2024. On the nature of explanation: An epistemological-linguistic perspective for explanation-based natural language inference. *Philosophy & Technology*, 37(3):88.

Marco Valentino, Ian Pratt-Hartmann, and André Freitas. 2021a. Do natural language explanations represent valid logical arguments? verifying entailment in explainable nli gold standards. In *Proceedings of the 14th International Conference on Computational Semantics (IWCS)*, pages 76–86.

Marco Valentino, Mokanarangan Thayaparan, Deborah Ferreira, and André Freitas. 2022a. Hybrid autoregressive inference for scalable multi-hop explanation regeneration. In *Proceedings of the AAAI Conference on Artificial Intelligence*, volume 36, pages 11403–11411.

Marco Valentino, Mokanarangan Thayaparan, and André Freitas. 2021b. Unification-based reconstruction of multi-hop explanations for science questions. In *Proceedings of the 16th Conference of the European Chapter of the Association for Computational Linguistics: Main Volume*, pages 200–211, Online. Association for Computational Linguistics.

Marco Valentino, Mokanarangan Thayaparan, and André Freitas. 2022b. Case-based abductive natural language inference. In *Proceedings of the 29th International Conference on Computational Linguistics*, pages 1556–1568.

Jason Wei, Xuezhi Wang, Dale Schuurmans, Maarten Bosma, Fei Xia, Ed Chi, Quoc V Le, Denny Zhou, et al. 2022. Chain-of-thought prompting elicits reasoning in large language models. *Advances in neural information processing systems*, 35:24824–24837.

Sarah Wiegreffe and Ana Marasovic. Teach me to explain: A review of datasets for explainable natural language processing. In *Thirty-fifth Conference on Neural Information Processing Systems Datasets and Benchmarks Track (Round 1)*.

Sarah Wiegreffe and Ana Marasović. 2021. Teach me to explain: A review of datasets for explainable nlp. *arXiv preprint arXiv:2102.12060*.

James Woodward and Lauren Ross. 2021. Scientific Explanation. In Edward N. Zalta, editor, *The Stanford Encyclopedia of Philosophy*, Summer 2021 edition. Metaphysics Research Lab, Stanford University.

Zhengnan Xie, Sebastian Thiem, Jaycie Martin, Elizabeth Wainwright, Steven Marmorstein, and Peter Jansen. 2020. Worldtree v2: A corpus of science-domain structured explanations and inference patterns supporting multi-hop inference. In *Proceedings of the 12th Language Resources and Evaluation Conference*, pages 5456–5473.

Zhilin Yang, Peng Qi, Saizheng Zhang, Yoshua Bengio, William Cohen, Ruslan Salakhutdinov, and Christopher D Manning. 2018. Hotpotqa: A dataset for diverse, explainable multi-hop question answering. In *Proceedings of the 2018 Conference on Empirical Methods in Natural Language Processing*, pages 2369–2380.

Shunyu Yao, Dian Yu, Jeffrey Zhao, Izhak Shafran, Tom Griffiths, Yuan Cao, and Karthik Narasimhan. 2024. Tree of thoughts: Deliberate problem solving with large language models. *Advances in Neural Information Processing Systems*, 36.

Yingji Zhang, Danilo Carvalho, and Andre Freitas. 2024a. Learning disentangled semantic spaces of explanations via invertible neural networks. In *Proceedings of the 62nd Annual Meeting of the Association for Computational Linguistics (Volume 1: Long Papers)*, pages 2113–2134, Bangkok, Thailand. Association for Computational Linguistics.

Yingji Zhang, Danilo Carvalho, Marco Valentino, Ian Pratt-Hartmann, and Andre Freitas. 2024b. Improving semantic control in discrete latent spaces with transformer quantized variational autoencoders. In *Findings of the Association for Computational Linguistics: EACL 2024*, pages 1434–1450, St. Julian's, Malta. Association for Computational Linguistics.

Yingji Zhang, Danilo S Carvalho, Ian Pratt-Hartmann, and Andre Freitas. 2023. Towards controllable natural language inference through lexical inference types. *arXiv preprint arXiv:2308.03581*.

Yingji Zhang, Marco Valentino, Danilo Carvalho, Ian Pratt-Hartmann, and Andre Freitas. 2024c. Graph-induced syntactic-semantic spaces in transformer-based variational AutoEncoders. In *Findings of the Association for Computational Linguistics: NAACL 2024*, pages 474–489, Mexico City, Mexico. Association for Computational Linguistics.

Haiyan Zhao, Hanjie Chen, Fan Yang, Ninghao Liu, Huiqi Deng, Hengyi Cai, Shuaiqiang Wang, Dawei Yin, and Mengnan Du. 2024. Explainability for large language models: A survey. *ACM Transactions on Intelligent Systems and Technology*, 15(2):1–38.

Wenting Zhao, Mor Geva, Bill Yuchen Lin, Michihiro Yasunaga, Aman Madaan, and Tao Yu. 2023. Complex reasoning in natural language. In *Proceedings of the 61st Annual Meeting of the Association for Computational Linguistics (Volume 6: Tutorial Abstracts)*, pages 11–20, Toronto, Canada. Association for Computational Linguistics.

Huaixiu Steven Zheng, Swaroop Mishra, Xinyun Chen, Heng-Tze Cheng, Ed H Chi, Quoc V Le, and Denny Zhou. 2023. Take a step back: Evoking reasoning via abstraction in large language models. *arXiv preprint arXiv:2310.06117*.

Zining Zhu, Hanjie Chen, Xi Ye, Qing Lyu, Chenhao Tan, Ana Marasovic, and Sarah Wiegreffe. 2024. Explanation in the era of large language models. In *Proceedings of the 2024 Conference of the North American Chapter of the Association for Computational Linguistics: Human Language Technologies (Volume 5: Tutorial Abstracts)*, pages 19–25, Mexico City, Mexico. Association for Computational Linguistics.

AI for Science in the Era of Large Language Models

Zhenyu Bi[1], **Minghao Xu**[2], **Jian Tang**[2], **Xuan Wang**[1]
[1]Department of Computer Science, Virginia Tech, USA
[2]Mila - Quebec AI Institute, Canada
[1]{zhenyub, xuanw}@vt.edu,
[2]minghao.xu@mila.quebec, [2]tangjianpku@gmail.com

Abstract

The capabilities of AI in the realm of science span a wide spectrum, from the atomic level, where it solves partial differential equations for quantum systems, to the molecular level, predicting chemical or protein structures, and even extending to societal predictions like infectious disease outbreaks. Recent advancements in large language models (LLMs), exemplified by models like ChatGPT, have showcased significant prowess in tasks involving natural language, such as translating languages, constructing chatbots, and answering questions. When we consider scientific data, we notice a resemblance to natural language in terms of sequences – scientific literature and health records presented as text, bio-omics data arranged in sequences, or sensor data like brain signals. The question arises: Can we harness the potential of these recent LLMs to drive scientific progress? In this tutorial, we will explore the application of large language models to three crucial categories of scientific data: 1) textual data, 2) biomedical sequences, and 3) brain signals. Furthermore, we will delve into LLMs' challenges in scientific research, including ensuring trustworthiness, achieving personalization, and adapting to multi-modal data representation.

1 Tutorial Content

The impressive capabilities of Artificial Intelligence (AI) within the realm of science span a wide spectrum, from the atomic level, where it attempts to solve partial differential equations for quantum systems, to the molecular level, where it accurately predicts the structures of chemicals and proteins, and extends even further, encompassing societal predictions like forecasting infectious disease outbreaks (Zhang et al., 2023a). Amidst this landscape of possibilities, recent advancements in large language models (LLMs), notably exemplified by models like ChatGPT[1], have risen to the forefront, demonstrating significant proficiency in tasks tied to natural language. These tasks include language translation, constructing chatbots, and answering questions (Yang et al., 2023).

Interestingly, when we turn our attention to scientific data, we discover a striking resemblance to natural language in terms of sequences. Scientific literature and health records are laid out as textual narratives, bio-omics data takes the form of molecular sequences, and even sensor data like brain signals is inherently sequential (Wang et al., 2021a; Thirunavukarasu et al., 2023). This observation prompts a compelling question: Can we leverage the potential of these advanced LLMs to propel scientific advancement?

In this tutorial, we embark on a journey to explore precisely this intersection—the fusion of cutting-edge large language models with scientific inquiry. Our exploration zooms in on three pivotal categories of scientific data: 1) textual data (Alsentzer et al., 2019; Singhal et al., 2022; Beltagy et al., 2019; Lee et al., 2020; Gu et al., 2021; Alrowili and Vijay-Shanker, 2021; Yasunaga et al., 2022), 2) biomedical sequences (Ji et al., 2021; Zvyagin et al., 2022; Fishman et al., 2023; Dalla-Torre et al., 2023; Nguyen et al., 2023; Yamada and Hamada, 2022; Yang et al., 2022; Chen et al., 2022; Zhang et al., 2023b; Rives et al., 2021; Bepler and Berger, 2021; Brandes et al., 2022; Madani et al., 2023; Lin et al., 2023; Zheng et al., 2023; Xu et al., 2023), and 3) brain signals (Wang et al., 2022a; Wang and Ji, 2022; Tang et al., 2023). By drawing inspiration from the transformative capabilities of LLMs, we seek to unravel novel understanding and innovation within each domain.

As we move forward, we further discuss the intricate challenges that accompany the infusion of AI into scientific research. The foundation of trustworthiness stands tall—how do we ensure the reliability of AI-enhanced scientific insights? The concept of personalization emerges as a critical

[1]https://chat.openai.com/chat

Proceedings of the 2024 Conference on Empirical Methods in Natural Language Processing: Tutorial Abstracts, pages 32–38
November 12–16, 2024.

consideration, urging us to tailor LLMs to the specific contours of scientific investigation. Furthermore, the multi-dimensional nature of scientific data beckons us to master the art of handling data representations that span across various modalities.

2 Tutorial Type

This is a **cutting-edge** tutorial, bridging the gap between the NLP community and AI for Science.

3 Target Audience and Prerequisites

This tutorial is intended for researchers and practitioners in natural language processing, machine learning, and their applications to science domains. While the audience with a good background in the above areas would benefit most from this tutorial, we believe the material to be presented would give the general audience and newcomers a complete picture of the important research topics in AI for science with large language models. Our tutorial is designed as self-contained, so no specific background knowledge is assumed of the audience. However, it would be beneficial for the audience to know about the basics of deep learning technologies and pre-trained language models (e.g., Transformer (Vaswani et al., 2017), BERT (Kenton and Toutanova, 2019), GPT (Brown et al., 2020), and T5 (Raffel et al., 2020)) before attending this tutorial. We will provide a reading list of background knowledge on our tutorial website.

4 Tutorial Outline

This tutorial is expected to be **3 hours** in duration plus a **30-minute break** in between. The contents are outlined below.

4.1 Background and Motivation [20 min]

We will first introduce the background knowledge of LLMs and the big picture of AI for Science. Then we will motivate the following topics of LLMs for science on three pivotal categories of scientific data: 1) textual data, 2) biomedical sequences, and 3) brain signals.

4.2 LLMs on Scientific Textual Data [40 min]

First, we introduce LLMs in the realm of scientific textual data, which encompasses diverse domains like biomedical literature (Beltagy et al., 2019; Lee et al., 2020; Gu et al., 2021; Alrowili and Vijay-Shanker, 2021; Yasunaga et al., 2022) and electronic health records (Alsentzer et al., 2019; Singhal et al., 2022). This form of scientific textual data closely mirrors the fundamental structure of large language models. It finds extensive utility across science and healthcare, facilitating tasks such as extracting valuable information and responding to queries. The applicability spans a multitude of areas, underpinning scientific and healthcare endeavors for information extraction (Wang et al., 2021b; Zhong et al., 2023; Wang et al., 2022b) and question-answering (Krithara et al., 2023).

4.3 LLMs on Biomedical Sequences [60 min]

Next, we extend the application of LLMs to the intricate realm of biological sequence data, where a rich landscape of possibilities emerges. Within this domain, we shift our focus to three distinct yet interwoven categories of biological sequences:

DNA sequences: From the blueprint of life, we draw inspiration as we delve into works such as (Ji et al., 2021), (Zvyagin et al., 2022), (Fishman et al., 2023), (Dalla-Torre et al., 2023), and (Nguyen et al., 2023). These pioneering endeavors pave the way for unraveling the secrets encrypted within the very essence of organisms. The DNA LLMs have a wide application in downstream tasks such as predicting regulatory elements for enhancers, promoters, epigenetic marks, and splice sites from DNA sequences (Grešová et al., 2023; Dalla-Torre et al., 2023).

RNA sequences: Navigating the intricate world of gene expression, we embrace the innovative contributions outlined in (Yamada and Hamada, 2022), (Yang et al., 2022), (Chen et al., 2022), and (Zhang et al., 2023b). These strides empower us to decode the symphony of biological processes orchestrated by RNA. The RNA LLMs have a wide application in RNA structure and function prediction (Yamada and Hamada, 2022; Zhang et al., 2023b), RNA-protein interaction prediction (Chen et al., 2022), and cell type annotation (Yang et al., 2022).

Protein sequences: Venturing into the complex realm of proteins, we are guided by luminous works like (Rives et al., 2021), (Bepler and Berger, 2021), (Brandes et al., 2022), (Madani et al., 2023), (Lin et al., 2023), (Zheng et al., 2023), and (Xu et al., 2023). These endeavors illuminate the path to unraveling the intricate choreography of molecular functions and interactions. The protein LLMs have a wide application in functional protein generation

(Leinonen et al., 2004) and protein structure prediction (Suzek et al., 2015).

Within these domains, the transformative capabilities of LLMs manifest in a myriad of high-impact downstream applications. From predicting molecular structures to forecasting molecule interactions, and from unraveling molecule functions to drawing poignant associations with disease progression processes, LLMs stand as beacons of innovation, guiding us towards a deeper comprehension of life's building blocks.

4.4 LLMs on Brain Signals [30 min]

Last, we delve into the fascinating realm of applying LLMs to the realm of brain signals. In this section, we start with the introduction of a pioneering pre-trained brain signal representation model, as detailed in (Wang et al., 2022a). Building upon this foundation, we further introduce an exciting topic of open-vocabulary brain-to-text translation (Wang and Ji, 2022; Tang et al., 2023). This intriguing endeavor involves training translation models to automatically decipher the intricate contents of individuals' thoughts, offering a captivating glimpse into the potential convergence of technology and cognitive processes.

4.5 Future Research Directions [30 min]

As a conclusion, we will take a closer look at the challenges that come with using AI in scientific research. One big challenge is making sure that the scientific insights enhanced by AI are reliable and trustworthy, including model explainability and interpretability, model robustness to adversarial attacks, model bias towards different populations, and data privacy issues. We also think about the idea of personalization, which means adjusting LLMs to fit the specific needs of different personalized data. For example, there is a large individual variance in brain signals when different people are thinking of the same word under the same context. Instead of using one LLM to fit everyone, can we construct personalized LLMs based on different brain patterns for different people? And since scientific information can be very varied, we learn how to handle different types of data in a skillful and effective way. For example, Google has announced Med-PaLM-2 (Singhal et al., 2023) that integrates image, text, and genome data in the electronic health record, declaring an expert-level ability for medical question answering. Can we develop more effective and efficient methods to integrate multi-modal and multi-omic LLMs into one powerful unified LLM?

5 Others People's Work

We will include a broad spectrum of other people's work that consists of **more than 60%** of the tutorial content (see References).

6 Diversity Consideration

We will discuss large language models scaled up to various scientific domains and various data formats (textual data, biomedical sequences, and brain signals). Our instructors consist of PhD students (Zhenyu Bi and Minghao Xu), junior faculty (Xuan Wang, Assistant Professor), and senior faculty (Jian Tang, Associate Professor). Our instructors also came from diverse geographical locations (Zhenyu Bi and Xuan Wang from Virginia Tech in the US, and Minghao Xu and Jian Tang from Mila - Quebec AI Institute in Canada). We plan to involve inclusive topics, accessible materials, diverse instructors, flexible formats, and targeted outreach to ensure a broad and varied audience engagement.

7 Reading List

We will provide a reading list of background knowledge on our tutorial website. A preliminary reading list can be found as the References.

8 Tutorial Presenters

Zhenyu Bi is a Ph.D. student in the Computer Science Department at Virginia Tech. His research area lies in the field of natural language processing, emphasizing real-world applications of Large Language Models. He is mainly interested in information extraction with weak supervision, especially text mining and event extraction; as well as fact-checking and trustworthy NLP. He received an M.S. degree in Intelligent Information Systems from Carnegie Mellon University in 2023, a B.S. degree in Cognitive Science, and a B.S. Degree in Computer Science from the University of California, San Diego in 2021.

Minghao Xu is a Ph.D. student at Mila - Quebec AI Institute, Canada. His research interests mainly lie in protein function understanding and protein design. He aims to understand diverse protein functions with joint guidance from protein sequences, structures, and biomedical text, especially boosted by large-scale multi-modal pre-training. He is also pursuing structure- and sequence-based protein design via generative AI, geometric deep learning and dry-wet experiment closed looping. He has given an Oral presentation at the main conference of ICML'23.

Jian Tang is an Associate Professor at Mila - Quebec AI Institute, Canada. His long-term interests focus on understanding the language of life (DNA, RNAs, and Proteins) with generative AI and geometric deep learning, with applications in biomedicine and synthetic biology. His group has developed one of the first open-source machine learning frameworks on drug discovery, TorchDrug (for small molecules) and TorchProtein (for proteins), and developed the first diffusion models for 3D molecular structure generation, GeoDiff (among the 50 most cited AI paper in 2022). He has given a few tutorials at international AI and data mining conferences including KDD 2017, AAAI 2019, AAAI 2022.

Xuan Wang is an Assistant Professor in the Computer Science Department at Virginia Tech. Her research focuses on natural language processing and text mining, emphasizing applications to science and healthcare domains. Her current projects include NLP and text mining with extremely weak supervision; text-augmented knowledge graph reasoning; fact-checking and trustworthy NLP, AI for science; and AI for healthcare. She received a Ph.D. degree in Computer Science, an M.S. degree in Statistics, and an M.S. degree in Biochemistry from the University of Illinois Urbana-Champaign in 2022, 2017, and 2015, respectively, and a B.S. degree in Biological Science from Tsinghua University in 2013. She has delivered tutorials in IEEE-BigData 2019, WWW 2022, and KDD 2022.

9 Estimated Audience Size

This is a cutting-edge tutorial that introduces new frontiers in the intersection of NLP and AI for Science. The presented topic has not been covered by ACL/EMNLP/NAACL/EACL/COLING tutorials in the past four years. It is hard to give an estimate of audience size given no similar tutorials have been delivered before. A rough estimate would be around **tens to hundreds of participants**.

10 Preferred Venues

We prefer the following venues for this tutorial: 1) ACL, 2) EMNLP, and 3) NAACL.

11 Technique Requirement

Standard equipment will be enough for our tutorial and we don't have specific requirements. We will bring our own laptop and a wireless pointer.

12 Presentation Materials

We will provide tutorial materials (e.g., tutorial slides and relevant list of papers) **one month** prior to the date of the tutorial. The tutorial materials will be **publically available** for open access.

13 Ethics Statement

Ethical quandaries frequently confront technological advancements, especially when it comes to dual-use scenarios where an innovation can bring both advantages and disadvantages. The tutorial introduces IE technologies, where the distinction between beneficial and detrimental employment predominantly hinges on data usage. Employing this technology responsibly necessitates the lawful and ethical acquisition of input text collections and other forms of input.

Regulations and standards establish a legal framework to ensure appropriate data utilization, granting individuals the right to request the removal of their data. In the absence of such regulations, the ethical responsibility falls upon technology practitioners to uphold righteous data use. Moreover, biases can infiltrate training and evaluation data, potentially diminishing system accuracy for under-represented groups or in novel domains. This bias can result in performance disparities based on attributes like ethnicity, race, and gender.

Additionally, systems trained on specific data can experience degradation when confronted with new, dissimilar data. This accentuates the need to thoughtfully contemplate matters of fairness and generalizability when employing IE technologies with particular datasets.

To guarantee the conscientious application of dual-use technology, a comprehensive approach involves prioritizing ethical considerations as foundational principles during every phase of system design. Transparency and interpretability should remain paramount across data, algorithms, models, and functionality within the system. Public verification and auditing can be facilitated by making software open source. Furthermore, strategies to safeguard marginalized groups should be explored as a part of ethical technology deployment.

Acknowledgement

Our work is sponsored by the Commonwealth Cyber Initiative and a generous gift from the Amazon + VT Center for Efficient and Robust ML.

References

Sultan Alrowili and K Vijay-Shanker. 2021. Biomtransformers: building large biomedical language models with bert, albert and electra. In *Proceedings of the 20th workshop on biomedical language processing*, pages 221–227.

Emily Alsentzer, John R Murphy, Willie Boag, Wei-Hung Weng, Di Jin, Tristan Naumann, WA Redmond, and Matthew BA McDermott. 2019. Publicly available clinical bert embeddings. *NAACL HLT 2019*, page 72.

Iz Beltagy, Kyle Lo, and Arman Cohan. 2019. Scibert: A pretrained language model for scientific text. In *Proceedings of the 2019 Conference on Empirical Methods in Natural Language Processing and the 9th International Joint Conference on Natural Language Processing (EMNLP-IJCNLP)*, pages 3615–3620.

Tristan Bepler and Bonnie Berger. 2021. Learning the protein language: Evolution, structure, and function. *Cell systems*, 12(6):654–669.

Nadav Brandes, Dan Ofer, Yam Peleg, Nadav Rappoport, and Michal Linial. 2022. Proteinbert: a universal deep-learning model of protein sequence and function. *Bioinformatics*, 38(8):2102–2110.

Tom Brown, Benjamin Mann, Nick Ryder, Melanie Subbiah, Jared D Kaplan, Prafulla Dhariwal, Arvind Neelakantan, Pranav Shyam, Girish Sastry, Amanda Askell, et al. 2020. Language models are few-shot learners. *Advances in neural information processing systems*, 33:1877–1901.

Jiayang Chen, Zhihang Hu, Siqi Sun, Qingxiong Tan, Yixuan Wang, Qinze Yu, Licheng Zong, Liang Hong, Jin Xiao, Tao Shen, et al. 2022. Interpretable rna foundation model from unannotated data for highly accurate rna structure and function predictions. *bioRxiv*, pages 2022–08.

Hugo Dalla-Torre, Liam Gonzalez, Javier Mendoza-Revilla, Nicolas Lopez Carranza, Adam Henryk Grzywaczewski, Francesco Oteri, Christian Dallago, Evan Trop, Hassan Sirelkhatim, Guillaume Richard, et al. 2023. The nucleotide transformer: Building and evaluating robust foundation models for human genomics. *bioRxiv*, pages 2023–01.

Veniamin Fishman, Yuri Kuratov, Maxim Petrov, Aleksei Shmelev, Denis Shepelin, Nikolay Chekanov, Olga Kardymon, and Mikhail Burtsev. 2023. Gena-lm: A family of open-source foundational models for long dna sequences. *bioRxiv*, pages 2023–06.

Katarína Grešová, Vlastimil Martinek, David Čechák, Petr Šimeček, and Panagiotis Alexiou. 2023. Genomic benchmarks: a collection of datasets for genomic sequence classification. *BMC Genomic Data*, 24(1):25.

Yu Gu, Robert Tinn, Hao Cheng, Michael Lucas, Naoto Usuyama, Xiaodong Liu, Tristan Naumann, Jianfeng Gao, and Hoifung Poon. 2021. Domain-specific language model pretraining for biomedical natural language processing. *ACM Transactions on Computing for Healthcare (HEALTH)*, 3(1):1–23.

Yanrong Ji, Zhihan Zhou, Han Liu, and Ramana V Davuluri. 2021. Dnabert: pre-trained bidirectional encoder representations from transformers model for dna-language in genome. *Bioinformatics*, 37(15):2112–2120.

Jacob Devlin Ming-Wei Chang Kenton and Lee Kristina Toutanova. 2019. Bert: Pre-training of deep bidirectional transformers for language understanding. In *Proceedings of NAACL-HLT*, pages 4171–4186.

Anastasia Krithara, Anastasios Nentidis, Konstantinos Bougiatiotis, and Georgios Paliouras. 2023. Bioasq-qa: A manually curated corpus for biomedical question answering. *Scientific Data*, 10(1):170.

Jinhyuk Lee, Wonjin Yoon, Sungdong Kim, Donghyeon Kim, Sunkyu Kim, Chan Ho So, and Jaewoo Kang. 2020. Biobert: a pre-trained biomedical language representation model for biomedical text mining. *Bioinformatics*, 36(4):1234–1240.

Rasko Leinonen, Federico Garcia Diez, David Binns, Wolfgang Fleischmann, Rodrigo Lopez, and Rolf Apweiler. 2004. Uniprot archive. *Bioinformatics*, 20(17):3236–3237.

Zeming Lin, Halil Akin, Roshan Rao, Brian Hie, Zhongkai Zhu, Wenting Lu, Nikita Smetanin, Robert Verkuil, Ori Kabeli, Yaniv Shmueli, et al. 2023. Evolutionary-scale prediction of atomic-level protein structure with a language model. *Science*, 379(6637):1123–1130.

Ali Madani, Ben Krause, Eric R Greene, Subu Subramanian, Benjamin P Mohr, James M Holton, Jose Luis Olmos Jr, Caiming Xiong, Zachary Z Sun, Richard Socher, et al. 2023. Large language models generate functional protein sequences across diverse families. *Nature Biotechnology*, pages 1–8.

Eric Nguyen, Michael Poli, Marjan Faizi, Armin Thomas, Callum Birch-Sykes, Michael Wornow, Aman Patel, Clayton Rabideau, Stefano Massaroli, Yoshua Bengio, et al. 2023. Hyenadna: Long-range genomic sequence modeling at single nucleotide resolution. *arXiv preprint arXiv:2306.15794*.

Colin Raffel, Noam Shazeer, Adam Roberts, Katherine Lee, Sharan Narang, Michael Matena, Yanqi Zhou, Wei Li, and Peter J Liu. 2020. Exploring the limits of transfer learning with a unified text-to-text transformer. *The Journal of Machine Learning Research*, 21(1):5485–5551.

Alexander Rives, Joshua Meier, Tom Sercu, Siddharth Goyal, Zeming Lin, Jason Liu, Demi Guo, Myle Ott, C Lawrence Zitnick, Jerry Ma, et al. 2021. Biological structure and function emerge from scaling unsupervised learning to 250 million protein sequences. *Proceedings of the National Academy of Sciences*, 118(15):e2016239118.

Karan Singhal, Shekoofeh Azizi, Tao Tu, S Sara Mahdavi, Jason Wei, Hyung Won Chung, Nathan Scales, Ajay Tanwani, Heather Cole-Lewis, Stephen Pfohl, et al. 2022. Large language models encode clinical knowledge. *arXiv preprint arXiv:2212.13138*.

Karan Singhal, Tao Tu, Juraj Gottweis, Rory Sayres, Ellery Wulczyn, Le Hou, Kevin Clark, Stephen Pfohl, Heather Cole-Lewis, Darlene Neal, et al. 2023. Towards expert-level medical question answering with large language models. *arXiv preprint arXiv:2305.09617*.

Baris E Suzek, Yuqi Wang, Hongzhan Huang, Peter B McGarvey, Cathy H Wu, and UniProt Consortium. 2015. Uniref clusters: a comprehensive and scalable alternative for improving sequence similarity searches. *Bioinformatics*, 31(6):926–932.

Jerry Tang, Amanda LeBel, Shailee Jain, and Alexander G Huth. 2023. Semantic reconstruction of continuous language from non-invasive brain recordings. *Nature Neuroscience*, pages 1–9.

Arun James Thirunavukarasu, Darren Shu Jeng Ting, Kabilan Elangovan, Laura Gutierrez, Ting Fang Tan, and Daniel Shu Wei Ting. 2023. Large language models in medicine. *Nature Medicine*, pages 1–11.

Ashish Vaswani, Noam Shazeer, Niki Parmar, Jakob Uszkoreit, Llion Jones, Aidan N Gomez, Łukasz Kaiser, and Illia Polosukhin. 2017. Attention is all you need. *Advances in neural information processing systems*, 30.

Benyou Wang, Qianqian Xie, Jiahuan Pei, Zhihong Chen, Prayag Tiwari, Zhao Li, and Jie Fu. 2021a. Pre-trained language models in biomedical domain: A systematic survey. *ACM Computing Surveys*.

Christopher Wang, Vighnesh Subramaniam, Adam Uri Yaari, Gabriel Kreiman, Boris Katz, Ignacio Cases, and Andrei Barbu. 2022a. Brainbert: Self-supervised representation learning for intracranial recordings. In *The Eleventh International Conference on Learning Representations*.

Xuan Wang, Vivian Hu, Minhao Jiang, Yu Zhang, Jinfeng Xiao, Danielle Cherrice Loving, Heng Ji, Martin Burke, and Jiawei Han. 2022b. Reactclass: Cross-modal supervision for subword-guided reactant entity classification. In *2022 IEEE International Conference on Bioinformatics and Biomedicine (BIBM)*, pages 844–847. IEEE.

Xuan Wang, Vivian Hu, Xiangchen Song, Shweta Garg, Jinfeng Xiao, and Jiawei Han. 2021b. Chemner: fine-grained chemistry named entity recognition with ontology-guided distant supervision. In *Proceedings of the 2021 Conference on Empirical Methods in Natural Language Processing*.

Zhenhailong Wang and Heng Ji. 2022. Open vocabulary electroencephalography-to-text decoding and zero-shot sentiment classification. In *Proceedings of the AAAI Conference on Artificial Intelligence*, volume 36, pages 5350–5358.

Minghao Xu, Xinyu Yuan, Santiago Miret, and Jian Tang. 2023. Protst: Multi-modality learning of protein sequences and biomedical texts. *arXiv preprint arXiv:2301.12040*.

Keisuke Yamada and Michiaki Hamada. 2022. Prediction of rna–protein interactions using a nucleotide language model. *Bioinformatics Advances*, 2(1):vbac023.

Fan Yang, Wenchuan Wang, Fang Wang, Yuan Fang, Duyu Tang, Junzhou Huang, Hui Lu, and Jianhua Yao. 2022. scbert as a large-scale pretrained deep language model for cell type annotation of single-cell rna-seq data. *Nature Machine Intelligence*, 4(10):852–866.

Jingfeng Yang, Hongye Jin, Ruixiang Tang, Xiaotian Han, Qizhang Feng, Haoming Jiang, Bing Yin, and Xia Hu. 2023. Harnessing the power of llms in practice: A survey on chatgpt and beyond. *arXiv preprint arXiv:2304.13712*.

Michihiro Yasunaga, Jure Leskovec, and Percy Liang. 2022. Linkbert: Pretraining language models with document links. In *Association for Computational Linguistics (ACL)*.

Xuan Zhang, Limei Wang, Jacob Helwig, Youzhi Luo, Cong Fu, Yaochen Xie, Meng Liu, Yuchao Lin, Zhao Xu, Keqiang Yan, et al. 2023a. Artificial intelligence for science in quantum, atomistic, and continuum systems. *arXiv preprint arXiv:2307.08423*.

Yikun Zhang, Mei Lang, Jiuhong Jiang, Zhiqiang Gao, Fan Xu, Thomas Litfin, Ke Chen, Jaswinder Singh, Xiansong Huang, Guoli Song, et al. 2023b. Multiple sequence-alignment-based rna language model and its application to structural inference. *bioRxiv*, pages 2023–03.

Zaixiang Zheng, Yifan Deng, Dongyu Xue, Yi Zhou, Fei Ye, and Quanquan Gu. 2023. Structure-informed language models are protein designers. *bioRxiv*, pages 2023–02.

Ming Zhong, Siru Ouyang, Minhao Jiang, Vivian Hu, Yizhu Jiao, Xuan Wang, and Jiawei Han. 2023. Reactie: Enhancing chemical reaction extraction with weak supervision. In *Findings of the Association for Computational Linguistics: ACL 2023*, pages 12120–12130.

Maxim Zvyagin, Alexander Brace, Kyle Hippe, Yuntian Deng, Bin Zhang, Cindy Orozco Bohorquez, Austin Clyde, Bharat Kale, Danilo Perez-Rivera, Heng Ma, et al. 2022. Genslms: Genome-scale language models reveal sars-cov-2 evolutionary dynamics. *bioRxiv*, pages 2022–10.

Human-Centered Evaluation of Language Technologies

Su Lin Blodgett[1]**, Jackie Chi Kit Cheung**[2]**, Q. Vera Liao**[1]**, Ziang Xiao**[3]
[1]Microsoft Research, Canada
[2]McGill University, Canada
[3]Johns Hopkins University, USA
sulin.blodgett@microsoft.com jackie.cheung@mcgill.ca,
veraliao@microsoft.com, ziang.xiao@jhu.edu

Abstract

Evaluation is a cornerstone topic in NLP. However, many criticisms have been raised about the community's evaluation practices, including a lack of human-centered considerations about people's needs for language technologies and technologies' actual impact on people. This "evaluation crisis" is exacerbated by the recent development of large generative models with diverse and uncertain capabilities. This tutorial aims to inspire more human-centered evaluation in NLP by introducing perspectives and methodologies from the social sciences and human-computer interaction (HCI), a field concerned primarily with the design and evaluation of technologies. The tutorial will start with an overview of current NLP evaluation practices and their limitations, then introduce complementary perspectives from the social sciences and a "toolbox of evaluation methods" from HCI, accompanied by discussions of considerations such as what to evaluate for, how generalizable the results are to the real-world contexts, and pragmatic costs of conducting the evaluation. The tutorial will also encourage reflection on how these HCI perspectives and methodologies can complement NLP evaluation through Q&A discussions and a hands-on exercise.

Type of Tutorial: Introductory

1 Tutorial Description

Designing effective evaluation methods for natural language processing (NLP) has long been challenging due to the complex nature of language, open-endedness of tasks, and multifaceted and context-dependent definitions of language quality. This challenge is exacerbated as "general" capability models (e.g., large language models) become more capable and prevalent. Not only must they be evaluated across a diverse range of tasks and domains, which can be difficult to define and validate, but their wide range of potential capabilities, including those potentially unanticipated by model developers (Ganguli et al., 2022), may also render evaluation results ungeneralizable to and unreliable in real-world contexts where the model is to be used.

Researchers have pointed out shortcomings of popular NLP benchmarks, metrics, and human evaluation methods (e.g., human ratings), such as their inability to capture nuanced meanings, their lack of validity, their perpetuation of biases and potential harm, and a lack of standardization and reproducibility (Howcroft et al., 2020; Clark et al., 2021; Jacobs and Wallach, 2021; Gehrmann et al., 2023). Ultimately, NLP models are to be incorporated into real-world applications, interacted with by people, and can have a profound impact on people's lives. Evaluation methods must take on a human-centered perspective that centers around people's needs, values, and interaction behaviors in order to produce results that can realistically reflect real-world performance and possible impacts.

These kinds of human-centered considerations are at the forefront of evaluation practices in social science where the validity of measurements is a key focus, as well as in human-computer interaction (HCI), a field primarily focusing on how to design technologies and evaluate the designs. In the past half-decade, HCI researchers have developed a "toolbox of methods" as different "ways of knowing" (Olson and Kellogg, 2014) people's needs, usage, and interaction outcomes with technologies. This tutorial aims to provide an introduction to these HCI perspectives and evaluation methods to inspire more human-centered evaluation methods in NLP, and to facilitate collaboration between the HCI and NLP communities.

This 3-hour tutorial will include 110 minutes of instructors' presentations followed by Q&A and a hands-on exercise. The presentations will start with a brief overview of current evaluation practices in NLP, including automatic evaluation and human evaluation. In this part, we will review common goals and assumptions that are built into existing

Proceedings of the 2024 Conference on Empirical Methods in Natural Language Processing: Tutorial Abstracts, pages 39–43
November 12-16, 2024.

evaluation practices. We also aim to highlight concerns and limitations—e.g., lack of reliability, realism, and standardization—which may lead to an overall lack of validity in the evaluation outcomes.

With these concerns and limitations of NLP evaluation in mind, we will introduce complementary perspectives in social sciences and HCI. We will introduce measurement modeling—a framework that disentangles what is measured (i.e., theoretical, frequently unobservable constructs) from how it is measured (operationalizations) and offers a rich vocabulary via *validity* and *reliability* to assess measurements (Jacobs and Wallach, 2021). We will further illustrate how these concepts can be applied to better assess NLP evaluation approaches (e.g., Xiao et al., 2023; Liu et al., 2024).

We will then provide an overview of common HCI evaluation methods, from human-subjects studies and surveys to analytical and simulated evaluations, and discuss the benefits and drawbacks of each. By comparing these different methods, we will particularly highlight the consideration of realism (McGrath, 1995; Schmuckler, 2001; Liao and Xiao, 2023)—designing evaluations in a way that the conclusion can be generalized to the real-world contexts where the technology will be used, and pragmatic costs to conduct the evaluation. Our goal is to inspire NLP researchers to explore diverse evaluation methods as alternatives to benchmarks and automated metrics, and develop human-centered evaluation methods with downstream human needs and lower adoption barriers (for people who should be doing evaluation, such as model developers) in mind. To further ground the introduction to HCI evaluation, we will present examples of HCI works conducting evaluations for language technologies such as chatbots (Langevin et al., 2021; Xiao et al., 2020) and writing support (Jakesch et al., 2019; Wu et al., 2019).

Lastly, the hands-on exercise will ask participants to work in groups to choose an evaluation method and design the details for a given use case. The exercise is designed to encourage participants to explore and compare different evaluation methods they learn from the tutorial, and facilitate further reflections and discussions.

2 Tutorial Content

2.1 Introduction and Background (10 min)

This section will motivate the importance of human-centered evaluation for language technologies, and why we believe valuable lessons can be learned from the field of HCI, which has a primary focus on evaluating and understanding human interactions with and impact from technologies.

2.2 Evaluation in NLP (30 min)

This section will review typical evaluation practices in NLP, and discuss how they may fail to inform real-world performance and usefulness because of a lack of human-centered focus. The goal of this section is not to be comprehensive about the wide range of metrics, datasets, and benchmarks in NLP, but to illustrate common assumptions in their design and application.

We will present examples of evaluation techniques, and ways to distinguish them (e.g., automatic vs. manual, or intrinsic vs. extrinsic). We will examine common motivations behind the development of new evaluations (e.g., to reduce costs or to evaluate a targeted type of model behavior).

We will present measurement modeling and the related concept of validity, and discuss ways in which measurements from the application of current evaluations can fail to exhibit validity, thus yielding unsupported conclusions.

2.3 Evaluation in HCI

2.3.1 Overview of HCI Evaluation Methods (40 min)

HCI researchers have developed and relied on a "toolbox of methods" to conduct evaluations of technologies. In this section, we will give an overview of common HCI evaluation methods (Barkhuus and Rode, 2007; Olson and Kellogg, 2014)—field studies, lab studies, surveys, and simulated evaluations—and discuss their benefits and drawbacks. We will highlight important considerations when making choices from the toolbox, such as quantitative v.s. qualitative, empirical v.s. analytical, and tradeoffs between realism and evaluation costs, which may depend on the types of claimed research contribution, technology development stage, and so on.

We will also include an orthogonal discussion about evaluation criteria commonly used in HCI research (MacDonald and Atwood, 2013; Hornbæk, 2006), including effectiveness, efficiency, user satisfaction, and other experiential and affective dimensions such as engagement and autonomy. Our tutorial will include a list of references for established scales and/or study procedures to evaluate these criteria. We will also touch on or provide references for practical considerations for evaluation studies such as human-subjects recruitment, analyses of results, and study design best practices as well as ethical considerations.

2.3.2 Case Studies (20 min)

After mapping the landscape of HCI methods, we will walk through two case studies of how language technologies are evaluated in HCI research, such as decades of work on chatbots and more recent work on writing support using LLMs.

2.4 Reflection and Open Questions (10 min)

In this section, we will reflect on current NLP evaluation practices through the lenses employed in HCI research regarding how to assess and select from different evaluation methods. We will discuss how the evaluation practices in HCI and NLP communities can complement and learn from each other. We will also pose open questions and suggest future directions for the community to work towards human-centered evaluation.

2.5 Q&A and Hands-on Exercise (20+50 min)

We will leave Q&A time for audience to directly engage with the instructors. In the last 50 minutes, we will ask participants to form groups and work on a hands-on exercise. The exercise will present participants with choices of case studies, which may include a type of language technology and an "effect of interest" of the technology on people. Participants will work in groups to choose an appropriate evaluation method and design the details. In the end, we will ask the groups to share their evaluation design and encourage collective reflection on common threads and challenges.

3 Expected Outcome

We plan to make the tutorial presentation materials public and the videos accessible to a wide population. With participants' consent, we may also share notes from the Q&A session and discussions in the hands-on exercise.

Expected audience size: We expect to have more than 100 in-person attendees, based on the audience size of a NAACL 2022 tutorial on human-centered evaluation focusing on explanation (Boyd-Graber et al., 2022), and the recent popularity of the topic of model evaluation.

Target audience and prerequisite background: As an introductory tutorial, our presentation will not assume any prior familiarity with HCI evaluation methods or the HCI literature more generally. We expect the audience to have some familiarity with common NLP tasks but not necessarily expert knowledge of NLP evaluation.

Technical requirements: We do not expect technical support beyond regular presentations. To encourage group discussions during the Q&A and the hands-on group exercise, we would like to request roundtables for participants.

Preferred venue: Due to the personal leave schedule of one of the instructors, we have a strong preference for this tutorial to be held later in the year at EMNLP 2024.

4 Diversity Considerations

Instructors: The instructors consist of researchers across NLP, HCI, and psychology at varying career stages, spanning both industry and academia, with equal gender balance.

Diversifying audience participation: The tutorial format is designed to encourage broad participation from researchers and practitioners across industry and academia; no prior familiarity with HCI methods is expected, and the presentation materials will be made publicly available.

5 Presenter Biographies

Su Lin Blodgett is a researcher at Microsoft Research Montréal. Her work has examined measurement and evaluation in NLP, and she has co-organized three editions of the HCI+NLP Workshop, a CHI panel on responsible language technologies, and a FAccT tutorial on measurement and NLP.

Jackie Chi Kit Cheung is an associate professor at McGill University and at the Mila Quebec AI Institute. His work has involved developing new evaluation methods and datasets for a range of NLP tasks including common sense reasoning, automatic summarization, and authorship attribution.

Q. Vera Liao is a principal researcher at Microsoft Research. She is an HCI researcher by training and recently works on human-AI interaction, explainable AI, and responsible AI. She taught tutorials at NAACL 2022, NeurIPS 2022, CHI 2023, CHI 2020, as well as various seminars internationally. She is frequently involved in organizing events (e.g. panels, workshops) that connect the AI and HCI communities.

Ziang Xiao is an assistant professor in the Department of Computer Science. His work lies in the intersection of human-computer interaction, natural language processing, and social psychology. Ziang is on the organizing committee and an associate chair for multiple HCI venues (CHI, CSCW, IUI). He co-organized the 3rd HCI+NLP workshop at NAACL 2024. He co-organized the first workshop on Human-centered Evaluation and Auditing of Language Models at CHI 2024.

6 Ethics Statement

We hope that our tutorial will inspire human-centered evaluation practices that may help alleviate potential harm and ethical concerns brought about by language technologies. As many of the evaluation methods we will present involve human participants, we will also address ethical considerations emerging from their application, e.g., risks and best practices surrounding human-subjects recruitment and study design.

References

Louise Barkhuus and Jennifer A Rode. 2007. From mice to men-24 years of evaluation in chi. In *Proceedings of the SIGCHI conference on Human factors in computing systems*, volume 10. ACM New York, NY.

Jordan Boyd-Graber, Samuel Carton, Shi Feng, Q Vera Liao, Tania Lombrozo, Alison Smith-Renner, and Chenhao Tan. 2022. Human-centered evaluation of explanations. In *Proceedings of the 2022 Conference of the North American Chapter of the Association for Computational Linguistics: Human Language Technologies: Tutorial Abstracts*, pages 26–32.

Elizabeth Clark, Tal August, Sofia Serrano, Nikita Haduong, Suchin Gururangan, and Noah A Smith. 2021. All that's 'human'is not gold: Evaluating human evaluation of generated text. In *Proceedings of the 59th Annual Meeting of the Association for Computational Linguistics and the 11th International Joint Conference on Natural Language Processing (Volume 1: Long Papers)*, pages 7282–7296.

Deep Ganguli, Danny Hernandez, Liane Lovitt, Amanda Askell, Yuntao Bai, Anna Chen, Tom Conerly, Nova Dassarma, Dawn Drain, Nelson Elhage, et al. 2022. Predictability and surprise in large generative models. In *Proceedings of the 2022 ACM Conference on Fairness, Accountability, and Transparency*, pages 1747–1764.

Sebastian Gehrmann, Elizabeth Clark, and Thibault Sellam. 2023. Repairing the cracked foundation: A survey of obstacles in evaluation practices for generated text. *Journal of Artificial Intelligence Research*, 77:103–166.

Kasper Hornbæk. 2006. Current practice in measuring usability: Challenges to usability studies and research. *International journal of human-computer studies*, 64(2):79–102.

David M Howcroft, Anya Belz, Miruna Clinciu, Dimitra Gkatzia, Sadid A Hasan, Saad Mahamood, Simon Mille, Emiel Van Miltenburg, Sashank Santhanam, and Verena Rieser. 2020. Twenty years of confusion in human evaluation: Nlg needs evaluation sheets and standardised definitions. In *13th International Conference on Natural Language Generation 2020*, pages 169–182. Association for Computational Linguistics.

Abigail Z. Jacobs and Hanna Wallach. 2021. Measurement and Fairness. In *Conference on Fairness, Accountability, and Transparency (FAccT)*.

Maurice Jakesch, Megan French, Xiao Ma, Jeffrey T Hancock, and Mor Naaman. 2019. Ai-mediated communication: How the perception that profile text was written by ai affects trustworthiness. In *Proceedings of the 2019 CHI Conference on Human Factors in Computing Systems*, pages 1–13.

Raina Langevin, Ross J Lordon, Thi Avrahami, Benjamin R Cowan, Tad Hirsch, and Gary Hsieh. 2021. Heuristic evaluation of conversational agents. In *Proceedings of the 2021 CHI Conference on Human Factors in Computing Systems*, pages 1–15.

Q Vera Liao and Ziang Xiao. 2023. Rethinking model evaluation as narrowing the socio-technical gap. *arXiv preprint arXiv:2306.03100*.

Yu Lu Liu, Su Lin Blodgett, Jackie Cheung, Q. Vera Liao, Alexandra Olteanu, and Ziang Xiao. 2024. ECBD: Evidence-centered benchmark design for NLP. In *Proceedings of the 62nd Annual Meeting of the Association for Computational Linguistics (Volume 1: Long Papers)*, pages 16349–16365, Bangkok, Thailand. Association for Computational Linguistics.

Craig M MacDonald and Michael E Atwood. 2013. Changing perspectives on evaluation in hci: past, present, and future. In *CHI'13 extended abstracts on human factors in computing systems*, pages 1969–1978.

Joseph E McGrath. 1995. Methodology matters: Doing research in the behavioral and social sciences. In *Readings in Human–Computer Interaction*, pages 152–169. Elsevier.

Judith S Olson and Wendy A Kellogg. 2014. *Ways of Knowing in HCI*, volume 2. Springer.

Mark A Schmuckler. 2001. What is ecological validity? a dimensional analysis. *Infancy*, 2(4):419–436.

Shaomei Wu, Lindsay Reynolds, Xian Li, and Francisco Guzmán. 2019. Design and evaluation of a social media writing support tool for people with dyslexia. In *Proceedings of the 2019 CHI Conference on Human Factors in Computing Systems*, pages 1–14.

Ziang Xiao, Susu Zhang, Vivian Lai, and Q. Vera Liao. 2023. Evaluating evaluation metrics: A framework for analyzing NLG evaluation metrics using measurement theory. In *Proceedings of the 2023 Conference on Empirical Methods in Natural Language Processing*, pages 10967–10982, Singapore. Association for Computational Linguistics.

Ziang Xiao, Michelle X Zhou, Wenxi Chen, Huahai Yang, and Changyan Chi. 2020. If i hear you correctly: Building and evaluating interview chatbots with active listening skills. In *Proceedings of the 2020 CHI Conference on Human Factors in Computing Systems*, pages 1–14.